CONFEDERATE BLOCKADE RUNNING
THROUGH BERMUDA
1861–1865

Courtesy of Mr. R. S. McCallan, St. George's, Bermuda.

The Blockade Runner—*Advance*

From a contemporary watercolor by Edward James.

CONFEDERATE BLOCKADE RUNNING
THROUGH BERMUDA

1861–1865

Letters and Cargo Manifests

Edited by

FRANK E. VANDIVER

THE UNIVERSITY OF TEXAS PRESS

AUSTIN, 1947

KRAUS REPRINT CO.

New York

1970

Reprinted with the permission of the Licensor
KRAUS REPRINT CO.
A U.S. Division of Kraus-Thomson Organization Limited

Printed in U.S.A.

In Memory of
CHARLES WILLIAM RAMSDELL

Table of Contents

Prefatory Note

At the generous suggestion of Mr. Frank E. Vandiver, I am happy to send a prefatory note for his book embracing some phases of the War between the States in which Bermuda played an active part.

As is well known, the blockade of Southern ports quickly brought into service a fleet of fast, low-lying ships called "Blockade Runners" which ran the gauntlet of the enemy's Navy carrying precious cargoes to the Confederacy.

In Bermuda this business centered at St. George's where the protected harbour is hardly more than a mile from blue water. Here, a local merchant, John Tory Bourne, was appointed Commercial Agent for the Confederate Government and it is his letter books together with those of Major Stansbury, Confederate Army, which provide some of the material for this volume.

The Bourne letters were recorded in tissue-leaved books by the water-copy method; some of them are so faded as to be almost indecipherable; in some others the ink has eaten through the thin paper so that the pages are in rags. Together they portray the activities of an enterprising, busy man engrossed in serious duties at a time of crisis. Running through the perfunctory, commercial language, one senses the atmosphere of urgency which was inseparable from his busy life. Frustration, disaster and success stand out from these yellowed pages penned by a man devoted to the Confederate cause.

There is only one thin, foolscap-size book of Major Stansbury's letters but this is in much better condition. The letters have been copied by an unknown, exquisite penman and are as clear today as when they were written.

About twenty-five years ago these books were in the possession of Charles Skinner Bourne, one of Mr. Bourne's sons, who despite complete blindness carried on a small, one-man grocery in St. George's. Bareness was the outstanding feature of this dismal shop. Outside the counter the room was empty except for possibly a barrel and a few boxes of canned goods.

The stock chiefly comprised such staples as flour, sugar and rice which was kept in barrels beneath the counter. When a customer appeared, Mr. Bourne would proceed to fill the order for, say, a pound of sugar in this manner: first the correct weight, selected by touch, was placed on the scale, then Mr. Bourne would scoop up some sugar and pour it into the pan on the other side of the scale, his left hand meanwhile touching the under side to feel when it began to fall. Having arrived at the correct weight he would give the customer a paper bag and tell her (for it was usually a woman) to fill it from the scale. Then coins would be exchanged which Mr. Bourne correctly identified by touch. On the shelves behind the counter there might be a few tins of canned goods or some bars of blue soap but there were always wide, blank spaces except for the far corner, near the outside wall where there was a dusty pile of old letter and account books.

I was able to do some small kindnesses for this poor, unfortunate man and thus became friendly with him. Sometimes, of course, he was defrauded by dishonest customers and he would recount these tales of robbery to me at considerable length. But we talked of other things too and as I was always interested in the past, I used to ask him to tell me about the days of blockade running in St. George's. Thus it came about that he let me look at these books and eventually sold them to me.

For the sake of history it was fortunate that he did so, for Mr. Bourne soon afterwards fell ill and died when his small possessions were scattered. If the books had remained in the store, I do not doubt but that these interesting records would have been thrown away as rubbish.

WILLIAM E. S. ZUILL

Editor's Introduction

The documents published in this volume illustrate a phase of the struggle of the Southern states to maintain trade with England, in spite of the Federal blockade, and keep their armies supplied with arms and munitions. Upon the availability of foreign supplies, largely depended the South's ability to carry on the war.

Confederate authorities were concerned with the problem of foreign supplies from the outset of the war. Jefferson Davis brought with him to the President's office his past experience as an army officer and as Secretary of War during Franklin Pierce's administration. He was sharply conscious of the appalling dearth of the war resources in the South. But on this subject he was stoically silent and busy. Not long after the provisional establishment of the Confederate States government, in February, 1861, Davis commissioned Raphael Semmes, late of the United States Navy, to go north to purchase supplies while that door yet remained open.[1] Semmes went to Washington, and New York, as well as to various New England cities, and succeeded in having considerable quantities of munitions sent South.[2]

This early bid for external supply was augmented in April, 1861, by the assignment of Captain Caleb Huse to service in Europe. He was particularly charged with the purchase of ordnance stores and artillery.[3] By the time Huse was sent abroad the Confederate Congress had become acutely aware of the blockade's potentialities. Characteristically excited, it questioned the War Department about measures taken to provide the Confederacy with assorted munitions. Leroy P.

---

[1]Jefferson Davis to Captain Raphael Semmes, Montgomery, Ala., February 21, 1861, in *War of the Rebellion: A Compilation of the Official Records of the Union and Confederate Armies* (Washington, 1880–1901. 130 vols., cited hereafter as *OR*), Series IV, vol. 1, 106–07; also, W. Adolphe Roberts, *Semmes of the Alabama* (Indianapolis-New York, 1938), 37–38.

[2]Roberts, *Semmes of the Alabama*, 38.

[3]*OR*, IV, 1, 220.

Walker, Secretary of War, replied to Congress that a competent agent ought to be sent to England immediately, apparently forgetting Huse.[4] Evidently Congress agreed with Walker, for on May 18 Major Edward C. Anderson was ordered to Europe to purchase supplies, not only of ordnance, but of all types. He was ostensibly to coöperate with Huse, but had authority to supercede him if it seemed best.[5]

While the government was concerning itself with the problem of the blockade, as well as the possible replacement of Captain Huse, that agent had been active. Arriving in Liverpool on May 10, he immediately made contact with the firm of Fraser, Trenholm & Company. C. K. Prioleau, a member of the firm, indicated that the company would do anything it could to aid the Confederacy. Huse, however, found that his letters of credit on Fraser, Trenholm & Company amounted to only £10,000, and that his letter from the Confederate Secretary of the Treasury, promising to honor his drafts up to $200,000, would have no value in commercial transactions. Then too, it took him only a short time to decide that there were no arms in the English market that would suit the Confederacy, though there were any number of muskets of indifferent quality. Belgium offered no better selection, so Huse turned his attention to manufacturing. He was much impressed with the Enfield rifle made by the London Armory Company, which had been making arms for the British Army, and wanted to contract with them for 10,000 arms. The British Government, though, would not release the company from its obligations and consequently no deal could be made at that time.[6]

Hampered by a shortage of funds on the one hand, and the small army of United States agents competing for munitions

---

[4]Walker to Howell Cobb, Montgomery, May 7, 1861, in *ibid.*, 292–94.

[5]Walker to Major Edward C. Anderson, Montgomery, May 18, 1861, in *ibid.*, 332–33; *id.* to *id.*, Montgomery, May 18, 1861, *ibid.*, 333.

[6]Huse to the Ordnance Department, London, May 21, 1861, in *ibid.*, 343–44; Anderson and Huse to Walker, London, August 11, 1861, *ibid.*, 539.

on the other, Huse almost entirely abandoned the open market and concentrated on contracts.[7] Added to these adverse
factors was the group of agents sent from the different Southern
States to purchase supplies on individual state accounts and
the resultant overlapping and conflict of effort.

Federal agents were doing well. They had money and their
very numbers gave them far better command of available
resources. Confederate agents tried France and Spain as well
as England and Belgium, looking for supplies, but found nothing to encourage them.[8]

Even so, Anderson and Huse purchased quartermaster and
medical supplies in addition to ordnance and in less than a
year had forwarded invaluable supplies to the Confederacy.
These supplies cost the Confederate States some two and a
quarter million dollars.[9]

Anderson, satisfied as to Huse's ability to manage foreign
purchasing, returned to the South in September, and Huse
continued his operations under considerably enlarged powers.
Walker wrote Huse that the victory of Johnston and Beauregard at Manassas should only lead the Confederacy to re-
double its efforts to obtain supplies. The magnitude of the
struggle caused Walker to add: "You are therefore hereby
instructed to increase your exertions and enlarge your operations for the object to the utmost extent of your power. To
this end you are authorized to depart, at your discretion, from
the terms of your original instructions."[10] A month later,
August 30, 1861, Walker wrote Huse that he should "operate
with a free and sure hand to meet our pressing needs, and

[7]Huse to Josiah Gorgas, Paris, July 22, 1861, in Letters Received by the
Confederate Secretary of War, 1861, document 3484, War Department,
Old Records Section, Confederate Records, National Archives, Washington, D.C. Microfilm copies of all letters from this collection are in the
writer's possession.

[8]Samuel B. Thompson, *Confederate Purchasing Operations Abroad*
(Chapel Hill, 1935), 15; Anderson and Huse to Walker, London, August
11, 1861, in *OR*, IV, 1, 539.

[9]Thompson, *Confederate Purchasing Operations Abroad*, 18–19.

[10]Walker to Huse and Anderson, Richmond, July 22, 1861, in *OR*, IV,
1, 494, Thompson, *Confederate Purchasing Operations Abroad*, 20.

ship safely, and consider your credit extended to the full of this demand."[11]

Accordingly, Huse, armed with immunity from interference by the Confederate commissioners,[12] went to work and began to arrange for a steady stream of supplies to go to the Southern armies. The problem of getting the supplies into the Confederate States had perhaps remained in the background during Huse's early rush to procure material. Now, however, he turned to it with determination, and contrived to start the *Bermuda* for Savannah—the first ship to go. She arrived in the Confederacy on September 28, 1861. Soon after, in October, the first ship to run the blockade solely on Confederate government account left England. The *Fingal* carried a cargo entirely composed of naval and military supplies, and reached Savannah on November 12.[13] Her cargo was desperately needed by the Southern forces and the 7,520 Enfield rifles consigned to the War Department were put to immediate use. One-half of them, 3,760, went to Albert Sidney Johnston's army, badly equipped and concerned with the defense of Tennessee. Louisiana received 1,000 rifles from the *Fingal;* Georgia got 1,100 and the Navy Department 1,000. The *Fingal* had on board some 17,000 pounds of cannon powder which was perhaps more desperately needed than the arms.[14] This shipment, with others that arrived about the same time, put Johnston's army in a much better condition to fight the battle of Shiloh.[15]

Meanwhile, as this trade grew and blockade running took on form and substance, a new problem began to emerge. The large "tramp" steamers which had been making the usual

---

[11]Walker to Huse and Anderson, Richmond, August 30, 1861, in *OR*, IV, 1, 594.

[12]*Id.* to *id.*, Richmond, August 17, 1861, in *ibid.*, 564–65.

[13]Thompson, *Confederate Purchasing Operations Abroad*, 19, 20. See Frank L. Owsley, *King Cotton Diplomacy: Foreign Relations of the Confederate States of America* (Chicago, 1931), 42, for British reaction to the voyage of the *Bermuda.*

[14]R. E. Lee to J. P. Benjamin, Coosawhatchie, S.C., November 23, 1861, in *OR*, I, 53, 190.

[15]Josiah Gorgas, "Ordnance of the Confederacy, I," in *Army Ordnance*, XVI (1936), 214.

runs from England to the Southern ports soon encountered a much too vigilant United States Navy and found it impracticable to try to reach Confederate harbors. Since the salient Union menace took the form of speedy ships designed especially for anti-merchant use, the South needed small, faster, craft. On the other hand, such vessels would be unable to make the lengthy trips from Liverpool or London to Wilmington or Charleston. The solution was simple: the large merchant ships continued to supply Southern needs, but they proceeded to Bermuda and Nassau instead of to Confederate ports. At these places, their cargoes were transshipped to swift, light-draft, blockade runners, which made the run to the coast.

Bermuda and the Bahamas were ideal as Southern entrepots. Geographical location, of course, made their selection obvious. Added to this advantage was the fact that the people in those colonies were sympathetic to the South. This feeling, in Bermuda at least, effervesced to the point of violence toward United States citizens, and extreme courtesy to Confederate commissioners and agents.[16] Such an attitude had been fostered by the forced removal of Confederate commissioners James M. Mason and John Slidell from the Royal Mail Steamer *Trent* in November, 1861, and diplomatic relations between England and the United States were strained almost to the breaking point. War was perhaps closer than is commonly believed. England was getting ready for it[17] and this, naturally,

---

[16]United States Consul Charles Maxwell Allen to his wife, St. George's, Bermuda, July 15, 1862. A typescript extract of this letter is in a collection of Blockade Papers, St. George's Historical Society, St. George's, Bermuda.

In explaining Bermudian feeling toward the South, Allen wrote his wife further: "I have once been attacked in my office and once knocked down in the street within a few days, the general sentiment is 'it's good enough for him, he's a damned Yankee.'" See *ibid*.

[17]Circular, the Duke of Newcastle, Principal Secretary of State for the Colonies, to Lt. Gov. Nesbitt of the Bahamas, Downing Street, December 14, 1861, in Governor of the Bahamas Letters Received from the Colonial Office File, 1823–1863, Government House, Nassau, New Providence. The Duke of Newcastle stated to the lieutenant-governor: "You have for

swung British public sentiment almost entirely in Confederate favor. At the same time, public sentiment in Nassau was further prejudiced against the United States by rigid restrictions placed on trade from the North to the Bahamas. The collector of customs at New York, acting on orders from Lincoln's Secretary of the Treasury, Salmon P. Chase, "prohibited the shipment of coals and dry goods and shoes, and quinine and other drugs and Tin Ware and Munitions of War, and sundry other articles to Nassau and the West Indies, and other foreign ports . . .," when he felt they were ultimately destined for Confederate consumption.[18]

---

some time been aware that two Gentlemen, Citizens of the Seceding States of North America have been forcibly taken out of one of the Royal Mail Steamers and conveyed to Boston by an officer of the United States Navy.

"Her Majesty's Government consider this proceeding to have been without justification, and they trust it may be so viewed by the Government of the United States.

"But as in the contrary event, it may prove impossible to avoid a rupture with that Government, I think it necessary to inform you that although in case of hostilities the powerful fleet of Great Britain will do all in its power to protect the commerce and secure the coasts of the British Colonies it will be impossible to increase the Land Forces now in the West Indies. . . ." He advised Nesbitt that it would be well for the colonies to make provisions for local forces and do everything else that would put them in a condition to repel attacks which the Navy could not prevent.

The editor wishes here to express his deep appreciation of the kindness and courtesy accorded him by His Excellency Sir William Murphy, Governor of the Bahamas. Through the Governor's good offices, the correspondence files of the Chief Executive during the American Civil War period were made available and other privileges accorded which place the editor deeply in debt to the Governor.

[18]Collector of Customs Hiram Barney to S. P. Chase, New York, June 12, 1862, copy in Governor of the Bahamas Letters Received from the Colonial Office File, 1823–1863, Government House, Nassau. The Acting British Consul at New York protested these restrictions to Her Majesty's Minister to the United States, Lord Lyons, who, in turn passed the protest on to Secretary of State William H. Seward. Seward took the matter up with Chase, who replied that "the restrictions on coal have been enforced by Collectors under my instructions of the 18th April last, alike upon domestic and foreign shipping clearing to Ports North

The gulf between the Governor of the Bahamas, Charles John Bayley, and the United States authorities widened as time passed, and in July of 1862 one of the British diplomats in Washington frankly told Bayley that "the United States Government is much irritated against the Bahama Islands, believing that the so-called Confederate States obtain their supplies and munitions of war principally from thence, and in the present state of public feeling in this country, I can only assure you that it will be an agreeable surprise to me, if I succeed in obtaining any relaxation of the present regulations in regard to trade with those Islands."[19]

It was natural that the Federal authorities should take particular notice of the Bahamas. Large export firms there, notably the house of Henry Adderley & Company, were engaged in handling cargoes for the Confederate government, and as yet the full potential of Bermuda had not been developed.[20] It remained for the valuable assistance rendered by such Bermudians as John Tory Bourne, commission merchant, and the strategic position of the port of Wilmington, North Carolina, in relation to Lee's Army to catapult Bermuda into a place of prime importance. Another factor, to be sure, contributed to the use of Bermuda as a large transshipment depot. As the following documents illustrate, yellow fever, curse of the tropics, scourged Nassau and the West Indies in the summer months. This disease practically paralyzed blockade running activity in those islands and Cuba, and operations shifted to the more northern islands.

Bermuda's importance grew rapidly as the year 1862 progressed. Blockade running expanded at an encouraging rate.

---

of Cape St. Rouge on the Eastern Coast of South America and West of the 15th degree of Longitude East.

"It will be my pleasure to remove all restrictions to trade when the present necessity which has made them imperative shall cease." Chase to Seward, Washington, June 14, 1862, copy in *ibid*.

[19] W. Stuart to Governor C. J. Bayley, Washington, July 19, 1862, in *ibid*.

[20] For an early case of Bahamian contraband litigation in which Henry Adderley & Company were involved, and British Foreign Office official opinion concerning it, see the Duke of Newcastle to Lieutenant Governor Nesbitt, Downing Street, October 15, 1861, and inclosures, in *ibid*.

From September, 1861, to February, 1862, only about 15,000 arms arrived in the Confederacy,[21] while 48,510 stands of arms arrived at Charleston, Wilmington, and Savannah during the period from April 27 to August 16, 1862.[22]

Confederate agents in the islands, particularly Louis Heyliger in Nassau, had been at work on the problem of transshipment, and he had reported to Secretary of War Judah P. Benjamin on December 27, 1861, that he had obtained "a very important modification of the existing laws, viz., the privilege of breaking bulk and transshipment. This . . . was not previously accorded. . . ."[23] John Bourne, in Bermuda, had not been idle. From his letter books printed in this volume, his operations can be easily traced—his handling of transshipment of supplies and cotton. The supplies went to the Confederacy; the cotton to Europe, where it functioned, on a limited scale, as the South's money. This medium of exchange—its full possibilities not yet realized—when put into the hands of Fraser, Trenholm & Company, soon passed to Huse's credit and he was able to use it in market and contract buying. He put it to such good use, and spent so much that the Chief of Ordnance, Colonel Josiah Gorgas, remarked that his "capacity for running in debt is the best evidence of the ability of Major Huse. . . ."[24]

The Confederate War Department wholly approved of Huse's assumption of authority to purchase supplies not specifically authorized in his instructions. Circumstances had

---

[21]Benjamin to the President, Richmond, February ?, 1862, in *OR*, IV, 1, 958; see also William Diamond, "Imports of the Confederate Government from Europe and Mexico," in *The Journal of Southern History*, VI (1940), 476.

[22]Gorgas Memorandum, August 16, 1862, in *OR*, IV, 2, 52.

[23]Heyliger to Benjamin, Nassau, December 27, 1861, in *OR*, IV, 1, 816.

[24]Gorgas to Seddon, Richmond, December 5, 1862, in *OR*, IV, 2, 227. Gorgas in writing of his career as Chief of Ordnance, after the war, said almost the same thing of Huse. He stated that the Major ran the ordnance department in debt for "nearly half a million sterling, the very best proof of his fitness for his place, and of a financial ability which supplemented the narrowness of Mr. Memminger's [Secretary of the Treasury] purse." Josiah Gorgas, "Ordnance of the Confederacy, I," in *Army Ordnance*, XVI, 213.

made it "judicious and proper" that he assume some authority, and the War Department's only concern was keeping him supplied with funds.[25] This was the only factor slowing him down—but it was doing an effective job. Although as was mentioned above, he succeeded in shipping a considerable number of arms and valuable accessory equipment, he undoubtedly could have obtained much more with the funds available to his northern competitors.[26] Though in straitened circumstances, Huse had, nevertheless, entered into a large business with the English firm of Saul Isaac, Campbell & Company, who had manifested a desire to help the South. This association soon brought grateful thanks from Benjamin, who wrote the company that he wanted to express the deep obligation felt by the Confederate government "for the kind and generous confidence which you have exhibited towards us at a moment when all others seem to be doubtful, timorous, and wavering."[27] This company rendered invaluable service to the South throughout most of the war.[28]

During this same period the woeful inadequacies of Confederate resources were becoming clearer to the chiefs of War Department bureaus. A system of priority was set up, in effect, and Huse was urgently told to send small arms and powder or saltpeter to the neglect of everything else, at the same time being advised that the South encountered such difficulty in sending bills abroad that the Treasury had resorted to making regular remittances in cotton to Fraser, Trenholm & Company. This plan seems to have been the one that Huse liked best, and certainly it produced results.[29] For some time an almost uninterrupted stream of supplies passed from Europe to the intermediate depots, thence to the Confederacy; but in June, 1862, losses of blockade runners started in earnest, including the *Ella Warley, Elizabeth,* and *Nassau,* though it

---

[25]Benjamin to Huse, Richmond, March 10, 1862, in *OR*, IV, 1, 985.

[26]Huse to Gorgas, London, March 15, 1862, in *ibid.*, 1004.

[27]Benjamin to S. Isaac, Campbell & Co., Richmond, March 17, 1862, in *ibid.*, 1007–08.

[28]See Thompson, *Confederate Purchasing Operations Abroad*, 30.

[29]Benjamin to Huse, Richmond, March 22, 1862, in *OR*, IV, 1, 1018; also Caleb House, *The Supplies for the Confederate Army* (Boston, 1904), 28.

is estimated that the ratio of successful voyages to captures during that year was seven to one.[30]

Perhaps the best evidence of the effective organization and administration of the blockade running business is the fact that on July 12, 1862, Colonel Gorgas wrote Benjamin's successor as Secretary of War, G. W. Randolph, that Huse's contracts, "with the supply now on the way will be a sufficient equipment for the troops & [I] propose to direct him to make no purchases of arms beyond that already made and contracted for. Other purchases of minor importance will still be needed, but involving no great outlay. I have already instructed him that artillery is of secondary importance unless of special character."[31] Huse advised that he needed some $255,000 to pay for 30,000 rifles delivered at Nassau, and for 45,000 in Vienna, along with several batteries of artillery, and for other purposes. Gorgas urged on Randolph the need for funds and Randolph, in turn, importuned C. G. Memminger, Secretary of the Treasury, to dispatch money to Europe. Randolph was particularly concerned on this point, as the "larger portion" of money already used had been advanced by S. Isaac, Campbell & Company "and we are anxious to refund to them."[32] This company had gone far out on a limb for the Confederate States. They had advanced money for almost all of Huse's purchases, and by the end of 1862 Huse had bought about $5,000,000 worth of supplies, mostly through this form. Remittances had far from kept up with disbursements, and in November, 1862, the Confederacy still owed the company about $2,000,000.[33]

While Huse, the War Department, and Confederate supply houses were feverishly buying and shipping supplies, and trying to pay for them, the Federal Navy had driven a wedge

---

[30]The ratio during 1861 had been nine to one. In 1863 it was about four to one, in 1864 three to one, and in 1865 one to one. See Owsley, *King Cotton Diplomacy*, 285; Diamond, "Imports of the Confederate Government from Europe and Mexico," *Jour. Southern History*, VI, 480.

[31]Gorgas to Randolph, Richmond, July 12, 1862, in Letters Received by the Secretary of War, 1862, document G. W. D. 438, Confederate Records, National Archives.

[32]*Ibid.*, indorsement by Randolph.

[33]Owsley, *King Cotton Diplomacy*, 392.

into the Southern line of communication with Europe. Nassau had become a point of concentration for the South Atlantic Blockading Squadron, which proceeded to make entrance and departure at that port virtually impossible for a time. In August, 1862, Huse, obviously alarmed, wrote Gorgas that "the port of Nassau has become so dangerous even as a port of destination for arms in British ships that I have thought it prudent not to order anything more to that port, for the present at least."[34] He added that since he was unaware of the presence of any Confederate government agent at Bermuda, he was selecting one to act there. Evidently Bourne's agency had not come under Huse's notice as yet, and no official agent, acting solely for the Confederacy, had been stationed in Bermuda. This was to come some four months later.

On December 5, 1862, Gorgas, summing up the operations of the Ordnance Bureau for the new Secretary of War, James A. Seddon, said that Huse had purchased, up to that time, 157,000 arms and large quantities of powder, some artillery, infantry equipments, harness, swords, percussion caps, saltpeter, lead and other items. He added that Huse had purchased, on his own initiative and "using rare forecast," large supplies of clothing, blankets, cloth and shoes for the Quartermaster Department. Payment for these supplies was still in progress, although remittances to Huse, at the time of Gorgas's letter, aggregated $3,095,139.18. This amount was totally "inadequate to his wants" and Huse was indebted for £444,850, or, considering the exchange value, $5,925,402 in Confederate currency.[35]

After this recapitulation of Huse's mission, Gorgas told the Secretary of War that further organization was contemplated at Bermuda. Major Norman S. Walker, sent to England with

---

[34]Huse to Gorgas, Liverpool, August 4, 1862, in Letters Received by the Secretary of War, 1862, document G. W. D. 733, Confederate Records, National Archives.

[35]Gorgas to James A. Seddon, Richmond, December 5, 1862, in Personal File of Josiah Gorgas, Adjutant General's Office, Confederate Records, National Archives. This letter is printed in *OR*, IV, 2, 227–28. In view of the figures involved, it is probable that the above enumerated supplies were those purchased with Isaac, Campbell & Co. funds.

$2,000,000 in Confederate bonds, was to return to Bermuda as resident disbursing agent and in conjunction with a certain S. G. Porter, Huse's agent, was to be in charge of cargo transshipments. Their business could start right away, since several valuable cargoes, routed under the new Bermuda plan, awaited transportation. Gorgas pointed out that it was "highly important that light-draft steamers should be purchased and used solely for the transportation of cargoes from Bermuda."[36] His advice was heeded, and so many fast ships were purchased from the Clyde river shipfitters in Scotland that the Edinburg *Scotsman* voiced the fear in November, 1863, that "there will soon be scarcely a swift steamer left on the Clyde."[37]

Bourne's letters and the cargo manifests will tell the story of how well the Bermuda agents got along, how effectively they carried on their work, and something of how they lived. Life in Bermuda took on a note of high gaiety as the blockade runners flocked to the islands. Mrs. Norman Walker maintained a perennial open house for the South's supporters and the Bourne's "Rose Hill," overlooking St. George's harbor, ebbed and flowed tides of Confederate agents and naval officers. The young girls of the islands arranged many social functions to which the young officers were invariably invited, and many of them were so fortunate as to receive invitations to some of the old homes on the islands. They found that "St. George's became not only a harbor of refuge, but a pleasant resting place after the excitement and fatigue of an outward voyage." Crates marked "merchandize" jammed W. L. Penno's warehouse, near the present offices of W. E. Meyer and Company. Kegs of "nails" and cases of "combustibles" filled J. W. Musson's warehouse, and that of Bourne, himself, bulged with gray cloth, shoes, blankets and commissary stores. St. George's, along with most other cities booming with war business, had its bad spots. The vast numbers of sailors crowding the streets of St. George's were out for a good time while on shore leave. They had plenty of money that came easily with running the blockade, and they were not afraid to spend it rapidly. Bermuda boasted excellent rum and many good places to drink.

---

[36]*Ibid.*

[37]Quoted in the *Nassau Guardian* (Nassau, N.P.), December 23, 1863.

St. George's offered, in addition, the diversion of the famous "Shinbone Alley," at the base of the road to Barrack Hill. Here the sailors could spend their nights and their money for all types of diversion, and consequently here they congregated. "Shinbone" with its iniquitous "dives," soon became, in the eyes of the old Bermudians, the most generally despised part of St. George's.[38]

Thus grounded in the islands, the new Bermuda plan, after initial organization and shakedown, began to produce results, as the documents here printed clearly indicate.

On the other hand, everything was not going smoothly with the agents in Europe. Major B. F. Ficklin, recently returned to the Confederacy from abroad, wrote Seddon on January 3, 1863, that he was personally convinced, from things he had seen and heard, that Huse was "*robbing* the Confederate Government in a most shameful manner." He admitted that it would be almost impossible to prove this imputation in a court of law, but he felt it his duty as a loyal Confederate citizen to bring this example of misconduct of a Confederate officer to the War Department's attention. Ficklin said that it was obvious to the Southern colony in Europe that Huse had no sentiments in common with the cause and had "the unblushing impudence to express himself in such a manner as to disgust all and lead to the inquiry why the Government should be thus imposed upon." On receipt of this charge, Gorgas stepped in to defend Huse, and said that he was so sure Ficklin had misrepresented the whole thing that nothing would be done unless ordered by the Secretary of War, and the matter seems to have been dropped.[39] This trouble was, however, the early rumbling of discontent among the Confederate agents

---

[38]See John Wilkinson, *The Narrative of a Blockade Runner* (New York. 1877), 143. This reconstruction of conditions in St. George's is based partly on the above cited source and partly on information furnished the writer, in conversation, by Mrs. Arthur Tucker, St. George's, Bermuda, to whom the writer would here express his sincere thanks.

[39]Major B. F. Ficklin to Seddon, Richmond, January 3, 1863, in Letters Received by the Secretary of War, 1863, document F. W. D. 9, Confederate Records, National Archives; *id.* to *id.*, January 10, 1863, in *ibid.*, and indorsement by Gorgas, January 17, 1863.

abroad. The main "blow-up" was not to occur until a year later, but already seeds of unrest were sprouting.

Meanwhile, the unfortunate policy being followed by the Confederate Treasury Department threw foreign purchasing operations into a state of aggravated confusion. Fraser, Trenholm & Company were instructed not to honor any drafts from Huse without a Treasury warrant for the amount. These took time to reach England, and as a consequence, Huse was not only out of money, but also deprived of means of obtaining any from government agents. At this crucial period, Major Norman Walker had arrived with his $2,000,000 in bonds, but the same attitude prevailed in regard to their disposition, and Huse had to hold them until sure they could be used without Treasury warrants.[40]

Even so, the energetic purchasing agent had achieved such results that Gorgas was able in February, 1863, to send an exhaustive list of stores purchased and shipped by Huse to the Secretary of War. The Chief of Ordnance enumerated 70,980 long Enfield rifles, 9,715 short Enfields, 354 carbine Enfields, 20 small-bore Enfields, 27,000 Austrian rifles, 21,040 British muskets and 2,020 Brunswick rifles secured by Huse. With cases, molds, kegs, and screw drivers, these arms were worth about £417,263. Shipments of artillery had been good: 129 guns of different types had been sent, with ammunition and spare parts, valued at £96,746 1s. 8d. The list goes on interminably with items bought and shipped, including percussion-caps, tools, serge, cartridge bags, lead, copper, shellac, tin plate, and steel. Total supplies shipped to February 3, 1863, were valued at £818,869 18s. 3d., while those in London, ready to ship, were worth £249,853 1s., and there were rifles and scabbards worth £117,750 awaiting payment in Vienna. Fraser, Trenholm & Company had received £613,589 credit, and this left £572,883 19s. 3d. due on the purchases.[41]

At the same time, in partial mitigation of the South's strained financial status, cotton was selling in England for a high of

---

[40]Huse to Gorgas, London, January 23, 1863, quoted in Gorgas to Seddon, Richmond, March 10, 1863, in *ibid.*, document G. W. D. 158.

[41]Gorgas Memorandum, February 3, 1863, in *OR*, IV, 2, 382–84.

21 and 22 pence a pound.[42] Thus "the necessity of the Confederacy to obtain credit abroad was met halfway by a great eagerness to obtain the staple."[43] Right in line with cotton's fantastic rise in value was Gorgas's order to his subordinates to secure this white gold for foreign shipment. The Ordnance Bureau, displaying its usual discernment, early realized the importance of blockade running on its own account and made the best use of limited facilities to bring in supplies. Other branches of the Confederate services of supply were not so acute in their vision, and consequently obtained proportionately less through blockade running.[44]

Huse's problems were confounded and multiplied while he was struggling for funds. Confederate soldiers were adept at expending lead, and the South's supply was not large enough to meet the consumption. Importations supplied the need for lead up to midsummer of 1862,[45] but heavy fighting subsequently strained resources. In March, 1863, the Superintendent of Confederate Ordnance Laboratories, John W. Mallet, wrote Gorgas that lead was so scarce that if a sudden emergency struck the more southern arsenals they would hardly be able to supply requisitions for small arms ammunition. He suggested, as a possible remedy for the shortage, that blockade runners be required to bring some fixed amount of lead as part cargo on every incoming voyage, to be paid for at a set price. He said further, that "the question of lead supply is nearly if not altogether as vital as that of niter, and such a demand upon the owners of vessels 'running the blockade' would seem no illegitimate exercise of authority at such

---

[42]John C. Schwab, *The Confederate States of America, 1861–1865; A Financial and Industrial History of the South During the Civil War* (New York, 1901), 33. This book is an excellent source for the history of Confederate financial policy, as is Owsley, *King Cotton Diplomacy.*

[43]Owsley, *King Cotton Diplomacy,* 387.

[44]Gorgas to Major R. M. Cuyler, Richmond, March 3, 1863, in *OR,* IV, 2, 416, for order concerning purchase of cotton. See also, Thompson, *Confederate Purchasing Operations Abroad,* 23.

[45]Major I. M. St. John to G. W. Randolph, Richmond, July 31, 1862, in *OR,* IV, 2, 30. St. John was Chief of the Niter and Mining Bureau.

a crisis as this."[46] On the same day, March 10, Major I. M. St. John of the Niter and Mining Bureau, was writing to Superintendent Mallet that one great factor in the shortage of lead was the tendency of blockade captains to throw it overboard when chased—two shipments having been lost in that way shortly before the date of his letter.[47]

A week later, Gorgas told Mallet that 500 tons had been ordered to Bermuda for shipment to the Confederacy. The firm of John Fraser & Company, Charleston, had also undertaken to bring some in at Government risk. Gorgas, in addition, had adopted a suggestion of Mallet's and distributed sporting percussion-caps to various points, to be exchanged for lead. It was recognized that the people were almost entirely unable to secure sporting ammunition, and would probably be anxious to trade for caps.[48]

Meanwhile, vitally important negotiations had been going on in Confederate diplomatic and financial circles abroad. John Slidell and Huse, together, had been discussing the possibility of a bond issue with the French banking house of Emille Erlanger & Company. During the period covered by the negotiations Confederate agents had proposed, and Mason had approved, the use of cotton warrants, calling for delivery of cotton at five pence sterling per pound, to pay for accrued indebtedness, and for additional supplies. Southern naval agents also were authorized to use some cotton warrants.[49] Arrival of definite information that a contract had been entered into between Erlanger & Company and the Confederate States, however, made the use of cotton certificates, or warrants, somewhat inadvisable, since the status of the Loan might be im-

---

[46]John W. Mallet to Gorgas, Macon, Ga., March 10, 1863, in Confederate Records, Chapter IV, vol. 28, 265–66, National Archives (these records will be cited hereafter as CS Recs., N.A.).

[47]St. John to Mallet, Richmond, March 10, 1863, in *ibid.*, vol. 5, 331.

[48]Edward B. Smith to Mallet, Richmond, March 16, 1863, in *ibid.*, vol. 5, 330; Mallet to Gorgas, Macon, Ga., March 10, 1863, in *ibid.*, vol. 28, 265–66.

[49]Thompson, *Confederate Purchasing Operations Abroad*, 54–57; James D. Bulloch, *The Secret Service of the Confederate States in Europe* (2 vols., New York, 1884), II, 220–27, for financial problems and operations of naval agents.

paired. But commitments had to be met in some way, and Southern financiers had to gamble.

Finally, on March 19, 1863, the books of the Erlanger Loan were opened for subscription in the principal European markets—Liverpool, London, Paris, Amsterdam, and Frankfurt. Final payment on the bonds was not made until October, 1863, and the total cash received by the Confederacy from the Loan does not seem to have been more than $3,000,000, though $6,800,000 may have been realized in various forms of credit.[50] Regardless of the exactness of this figure, the Loan was inadequate to the needs of the purchasing agents and the government. The resultant monetary chaos opened the way for a whole new financial organization abroad. Colin J. McRae, appointed Confederate special agent for the Erlanger Loan, tried desperately to mend the unravelling fabric of foreign buying. After his arrival in Europe, May 13, 1863, he worked toward rapid redemption of the Erlanger bonds, on the theory that this would best benefit the Confederacy's credit. Some Erlanger bonds were used in paying half of Huse's $2,500,000 debt to Isaac, Campbell & Company. The value of these bonds crashed after the news of Vicksburg and this company, later found to be keeping a double set of books on Confederate accounts, stood to be wiped out.[51]

Before McRae took hold in Europe, and before the Confederate Congress legislated a new economic order for the foreign commerce of the Confederacy, much had been done abroad and in the islands to keep open Southern lines of supply. During the period from September 30, 1862, to September 30, 1863, some 113,504 small arms had been imported, plus "large quantities of saltpeter, lead, cartridges, percussion-caps, flannel and paper for cartridges, leather, hardware, &c. . . ."[52] This number compared with 35,000 arms manufactured in the

---

[50]The amount of cash actually realized by the Confederacy has been variously estimated at $3,000,000 and $2,599,000. See Thompson, *Confederate Purchasing Operations Abroad*, 64, 71, and Owsley, *King Cotton Diplomacy*, 404. Thompson is the source for the statement that $6,800,000 worth of credit may have been received.

[51]Thompson, *Confederate Purchasing Operations Abroad*, 59, 65, 69; Owsley, *King Cotton Diplomacy*, 405.

[52]Gorgas to Seddon, Richmond, November 15, 1863, in *OR*, IV, 2, 956.

various armories of the Confederacy in the same year.[53] In other words, blockade running supplied more than three times the number of arms produced by home manufacture. When, by the end of 1863 and spring of 1864, the need for munitions and arms had eased somewhat, due to increased home production, the South found that the supply of food and clothing was alarmingly scant. The Confederacy's need for these two requisites never lessened, and, in fact, progressively increased. Huse was the chief purchaser of clothing as well as arms for a long time, and up to February, 1863, had purchased and shipped 74,006 pairs of boots, 62,025 blankets, 78,520 yards of cloth, 8,675 greatcoats, 8,250 pairs of trousers, 170,724 pairs of socks, 6,703 shirts, 17,894 yards of flannel and 97 packages of trimmings. Even so, the Quartermaster General was desperate for supplies, and told Norman Walker that the need of "blankets, shoes, and heavy cloth for overcoats" was so acute that all means should be used to obtain them.[54] He also wrote General Lee that the main reliance for a winter's supply of shoes, blankets and leather was blockade running.[55]

Perhaps the very desperation of the Quartermaster General brought results, for from November 1, 1863, to December 4, 1864, about 550,000 pairs of shoes and boots had reached the Confederacy, along with 316,000 blankets. From October 25 to December 7, 1864, 48 bales of cloth, 62 bales of shorts, 47 bales of flannel, one case of spool cloth, seven cases of silk, two bales of canvas, seven cases of woolens, twelve bales of hosiery, two bales of caps, nine cases of buttons, one cask of buckles and six cases of thread arrived at Wilmington and Charleston on government account.[56]

---

[53]*Ibid.*, 957.

[54]Gorgas Memorandum, February 3, 1863, in *OR*, IV, 2, 383; Quartermaster General Alexander R. Lawton to N. S. Walker, Richmond, October 13, 1863, in *ibid.*, 873; also Diamond, "Imports of the Confederate Government from Europe and Mexico," in *Jour. Southern History*, VI, 489.

[55]Diamond, "Imports of the Confederate Government from Europe and Mexico," in *Jour. Southern History*, VI, 489.

[56]George A. Trenholm to the President, Richmond, December 12, 1864, in *OR*, IV, 3, 955–58; Diamond, "Imports of the Confederate Government from Europe and Mexico," in *Jour. Southern History*, VI, 497. The table of arrivals given in Trenholm's report to the President is informative.

The third major item of army supply, food, was a pressing problem for Confederate authorities all through the war. Here and there in the Southern States, there were contrasted shortage and abundance of foodstuffs. Maldistribution, sharply accentuated by the wretched condition of the Confederate railroad system, constantly produced a shortage of food in the armies.[57] Various factors, particularly the fall of Vicksburg and loss of communication with the Trans-Mississippi Department, forced a meat shortage on the Commissary Department in late July, 1863. Frantic efforts to provide a supply from abroad succeeded in getting 8,632,000 pounds of meat into the Confederacy from November 1, 1863, to December 8, 1864, on government account.[58] About 520,000 pounds of coffee arrived during the same period.

Complicating the problem of a foreign supply of meat was the fact that blockade running firms were prone to leave this commodity accumulating and spoiling in the islands, and take aboard some other less bulky, and more lucrative, cargo.[59] Medicine, drugs, and salt, in addition to other myriad necessities, were imported from abroad in varying and inestimable quantities.[60]

In the meantime, and still before McRae's new plan was in operation, Huse had been wrestling with purchases of all types of supplies. He had rendered valuable service to the Quartermaster Department, though he had spent a great deal of that

---

[57]For an excellent account of the condition of Confederate railroads, see Charles W. Ramsdell, "The Confederate Government and the Railroads," in *The American Historical Review*, XXII (1917), 794–810. For some Confederate food shortages, see Frank E. Vandiver, "Texas and the Confederate Army's Meat Problem," in *Southwestern Historical Quarterly*, XLVII (1944), 225–33, and "The Food Supply of the Confederate Armies, 1865," in *Tyler's Quarterly Historical and Genealogical Magazine*, XXVI (1944), 77–89.

[58]Seddon to the President, Richmond, December 10, 1864, in *OR*, IV, 3, 930.

[59]Commissary General L. B. Northrop to Seddon, Richmond, December 12, 1864, in *OR*, IV, 3, 931.

[60]See Diamond, "Imports of the Confederate Government from Europe and Mexico," in *Jour. Southern History*, VI, 495–96, for some discussion of these imports.

agency's money. But the animosity of Quartermaster General Alexander R. Lawton and the ill feeling pervading the group of foreign agents, caused him to ask, and receive, release from the purchase of all but ordnance and medical supplies in May, 1863.[61]

During the same month a growing storm over Huse's actions broke with fury. The Quartermaster General, the Secretary of War, Commissioner Mason and others, regarded Huse, if not as a traitor, at least as cheating the Confederacy.[62] Huse had, however, a fairly strong lobby in his favor. Throughout the controversy over the purchasing agent's motives and honesty, he retained the confidence of Commissioner Slidell, Gorgas, and S. P. Moore, the Surgeon General.[63] The investiga-

---

[61]Gorgas to Seddon, Richmond, May 22, 1863, in *OR*, IV, 2, 564. Gorgas, commenting on the high rates paid by Huse, told Seddon: "I am free to admit that if Major H. had applied to me for instructions as to whether he should procure supplies at such rates, authority to that effect would have been given to him without a moment's hesitation. Purchases made at those rates have saved my department and that of the Quartermaster-General millions of dollars if compared with the charges made by Confederate houses at Confederate ports. . . .

"The matter of Major Huse's unfitness for making purchases is assumed by the Quartermaster-General probably on the testimony of Major Ferguson. I think it proper to say that I am perfectly satisfied with his business capacities, and so far as that is concerned desire no change."

[62]Thompson, *Confederate Purchasing Operations Abroad*, 27 ff.; Myers to Seddon, Richmond, May 16, 1863, in *OR*, IV, 2, 555–56; Seddon to Col. James R. Crenshaw, Richmond, May 23, 1863, in *ibid.*, 567.

[63]Gorgas to Seddon, Richmond, May 22, 1863, in *OR*, IV, 2, 564, pointing out the valuable services of Huse; Slidell to C. J. McRae, Paris, February 14, 1864, in *ibid.*, 3, 158, stating that Huse impressed him as being "animated by an anxious desire to perform most scrupulously and consistently the duties entrusted to him"; Emilie V. Erlanger to McRae, Paris, February 13, 1864, in *ibid.*, 158, saying "when in our early negotiations about the loan we desired Major Huse to take out the proposition for the Confederate States (which he was willing to do), and offered him for the danger he would be exposed to by running the blockade a compensation, he declined it, saying that in his capacity as a Confederate officer he thought he had no right to accept it.

"A man's character is easily stained by false assertions, and I think it a duty to establish truth whenever to my knowledge false statements have been made."

tion of Huse's activities, ordered by the Secretary of War,[64] terminated over a year later in his being acquitted of "any charge of intentional error and of any malfeasance of any kind," and with a recommendation for a raise in his pay.[65]

While this intra-agency contention was flashing back and forth, the Confederacy was becoming pitifully dependent on the ships running from the island transshipment depots. The shortage of ordnance stores, which had been partially alleviated for a time, returned suddenly. Southern arsenals engaged in the manufacture of small arms cartridges were faced with absolute exhaustion of the lead supply as 1863's summer steamed on and winter approached.[66] The supply remained short, and on October 9, 1863, Mallet wrote Gorgas that the first installments of lead ordered from Europe arrived just in time to prevent "a general suspension of work on small-arm's cartridges, but this stock is rapidly becoming exhausted, and I cannot learn that any further amounts are on the way to

[64]Seddon to W. G. Crenshaw, Richmond, June 21, 1863, OR, IV, 2, 600.

[65]J. A. Campbell to Seddon [Richmond], April 20, 1864, in OR, IV, 3, 704; C. J. McRae and M. H. Bloodgood to Seddon, Paris, October 1, 1864, in ibid., 703.

[66]Mallet to Gorgas, Macon, July 14, 1863, in CS Recs., N. A., Chap. IV, vol. 24, 202; Heyliger to Seddon, Nassau, July 14, 1863, in OR, IV, 2, 634; Mallet to Gorgas, Macon, August 15, 1863, CS Recs., N.A., Chap. IV, vol. 24, 252, recommending the order of an additional 1,000 pounds of lead from Europe since all arsenals except Richmond were dependent on that source; id. to id., Macon, September 7, 1863, ibid., 305, saying: "Lead we must import, and largely, as no arsenal—except Richmond—can otherwise be depended on for small arm's ammunition"; id. to id., Macon, September 11, 1863, ibid., 319–20, stating that out of 200,000 pounds of lead received at Augusta from foreign sources, only 69,604 pounds were still on hand. About 40,000 pounds had been used there and the rest sent to different arsenals over the period July 1 to September 7, 1863. It appeared to Mallet, in view of this, that only about 100 tons of lead had arrived out of the 1,100 tons ordered and 500 or 600 tons said to be already in Bermuda. He added: "The supplies to the four arsenals (Atlanta, Selma, Macon and Columbus) will scarcely suffice for one month's active work, and the amount still on hand at Augusta (about 70,000 lbs.) is estimated as sufficient for but two month's work there."

Augusta or this place."[67] Conversely, another of the ordnance department's outstanding necessities, saltpeter, was coming in fairly regularly. The cargo manifests which follow may give some insight into the reasons for the steady importation of saltpeter. Very few blockade runners ran to the Confederate States without some saltpeter as a portion of their cargo. Records indicate that between November 1, 1863, and December 8, 1864, 1,933,000 pounds of this vital component of powder had entered Wilmington and Charleston. During this same period 1,507,000 pounds of lead reached the Confederacy.[68]

This increased volume of ordnance and other supplies running to the Southern coast caused the Chief of Ordnance, the officer primarily in charge of government blockade running in view of the ordnance department's ownership of five blockade runners,[69] to change his departmental organization. The Ordnance Bureau's ships—*Cornubia, R. E. Lee, Merrimac,* and *Phantom*—had been running almost a regular packet service between the islands and Southern ports. Gorgas noted that up to August 2, 1863, his ships had made some fifty trips out and back without a single loss.[70] These numerous trips forced the first of the departmental changes. Major Smith Stansbury was assigned to the command of an ordnance depot in Bermuda, to handle ordnance and ordnance stores. He left for his new post in June, 1863.[71] A month later the Ordnance Bureau's organization underwent further change. Blockade running had assumed such magnitude and importance that Gorgas was unable, personally, to supervise its operations. He delegated this duty to his brother-in-law, Major Thomas L. Bayne, appointed "immediate representative of the War Department in all that pertains to the running and management

---

[67]Mallet to Gorgas, Macon, October 9, 1863, CS Recs., N.A., Chap. IV, vol. 24, 479.

[68]Seddon to the President, Richmond, December 10, 1864, *OR*, IV, 3, 930.

[69]Seddon to Col. James R. Crenshaw, Richmond, May 23, 1863, *ibid.*, 2, 567.

[70]Gorgas to Seddon, Richmond, November 15, 1863, *OR*, IV, 2, 955; Entry of August 2, 1863, in *The Civil War Diary of General Josiah Gorgas* (Frank E. Vandiver, editor, Tuscaloosa, Ala., 1947).

[71]*Ibid.*, June 18, 1863.

of Steamers. . . . He will also be charged with the general management of the Government Steamers under the directions of the Chief of Ordnance. . . ."[72] Thus, somewhat streamlined, the Confederate government's blockade enterprises, public and private, worked through 1863. Further important changes were not to be made until March, 1864.

But while the Confederacy was busy working on ways and means to obtain supplies from abroad, the blockade had been affecting the West Indies in numerous ways. Governor Bayley, in an address to the Legislative Council and House of Assembly of the Bahamas, commented on the magnitude of the Civil War in March, 1863. He pointed out, though it was superfluous to do so, that the Colony's location made it the resort of blockade runners. Under the protection of the mother country, he said, the colonials enjoyed the "right of engaging in commercial operations with each or either of the belligerents." He indicated that, while the United States had been, and still remained, annoyed by West Indian commerce with the Confederacy, "the people of the Northern States have awakened to a sense of their inconsistency and injustice, and that while they have not ceased to complain of the inconvenience to which they are subjected by the Neutral commerce of these islands, they have ceased to reprobate as moral delinquencies practices which derive their greatest anthority from the example originally set by themselves." Though American naval officers "may have orders not to abate one jot of their just belligerent rights, they are instructed to abstain scrupulously from acts of wanton provocation or offensive discourtesy within the prescriptive jurisdiction of a friendly Power."[73]

Bayley's speech seems to have caused unfavorable comment in the United States, and it most certainly did not suit Down-

[72]Special Orders Number 174, Adjutant and Inspector General's Office, Richmond, July 23, 1863, in Personal File of Thomas L. Bayne, Confederate Records, Adjutant General's Office, National Archives.

[73]Speech of Governor Charles John Bayley to the Bahamian House of Assembly, March 2, 1863, in *Votes of the Honorable House of Assembly of the Bahama Islands, Session Commencing on the 2nd day of March, and ending on the 26th day of May, 1863* (Nassau, N.P.), 2–3.

ing Street. On April 11, 1863, the Duke of Newcastle wrote the Governor that his address was at hand, and said:

> I am obliged to inform you that I can by no means approve that part of your speech in which you allude to the practice of despatching vessels from Nassau to the blockaded ports of the Confederate States.
>
> It is perfectly true that the British Government is not bound to interfere in order to repress or even to discountenance this practice; just as the British Government is not bound to interfere with operations carried on by British subjects in violation of the Revenue Laws of a Foreign Country.
>
> But it is undoubted that a Belligerent has a right to blockade the ports of his enemy [Bayley wrote in the margin: "I never said he had not"]— that a breach of blockade is an invasion of that right [Bayley commented: "Did I deny this?"],—and that the Power whose belligerent rights are thus violated may reasonably complain that Her Majesty's Representative speaking publicly in his official capacity should refer to proceedings thus injurious to its interests in a tone of encouragement or protection [Bayley remarked: "Hah"].
>
> I have no doubt the language which you used was very acceptable to the inhabitants of the Colony, who are naturally anxious to make the most of their present position relatively to the Seat of War. But I think you failed to observe that in using it, you were laying yourself open to a charge of unfriendly conduct towards a neighboring power, and were impairing the position of the Government which you serve.[74]

Though Bayley apparently tried to straighten out this unpleasantness and correct Downing Street's misinterpretations in a letter to Newcastle on May 5, he seems only to have protracted the contention. The Secretary for the Colonies wrote him on June 6 that his letter had not removed any objections to his speech. The Duke added, firmly:

> I think it best to instruct you that whatever opinions you may individually entertain on the points to which you advert, what is expected of you is that you will not without urgent occasion or without authority express opinions affecting the relations of Her Majesty's Government with foreign Governments and Countries, and that you will abstain from adopting a tone and spirit in alluding to invasions of the right of blockade which even as construed and explained by yourself is in an officer occupying

---

[74]Duke of Newcastle to Bayley, Downing Street, April 11, 1863, in Governor of the Bahamas Letters Received from the Colonial Office File, 1823–1863, Government House, Nassau.

your position unjustifiable and cannot but be injurious to this country in its relations with the United States.[75]

Bayley's tenure of office lasted for another year, during which time little trouble was encountered by Confederate agents operating in the islands. After Bayley's replacement in December, 1864, by Rawson W. Rawson, Confederate fortune waned in the Bahamas.

But to return to the adoption of the new plan of buying and shipping supplies developed earlier in this year: on March 17, 1864, Gorgas's bureau organization sustained a major alteration. Thomas L. Bayne, now a lieutenant-colonel, was relieved from duty with the Chief of Ordnance and assigned to special service under direction of the Secretary of War. His orders placed him in charge of everything concerning cotton exports and with "superintendance so far as pertains to the War Department of the importation of supplies from the Islands, and the provision of cotton to pay for all supplies purchased by the various Bureaus of the War Department, the payment for which is to be made in cotton."[76] The new regulations, based on a plan of C. J. McRae's, were put into law. First of these blockade statutes was "An Act to prohibit the importation of luxuries, or of articles not necessaries or of common use,"[77] which imposed heavy penalties for importing other than necessary goods. The second act concerning reorganization of foreign intercourse was "A bill [sic] to impose regulations upon the foreign commerce of the Confederate States to provide for the public defence."[78] This act placed the exportation of cotton and tobacco entirely in the hands of the government and the separate States of the Confederacy, and also imposed heavy penalties for violations. The President was authorized to use military units to enforce this law, and every effort was made to make ironclad the regulations promulgated

---

[75]Duke of Newcastle to Bayley, Downing Street, June 6, 1863, in *ibid*.

[76]Special Orders Number 64, A. & I. G. O., Richmond, March 17, 1864, in Personal File of Thomas L. Bayne, Confederate Records, Adjutant General's Office, National Archives.

[77]See James M. Matthews, ed., *Statutes at Large of the Confederate States of America*, 1 Congress, Statute IV, Chapter XXIII, approved February 6, 1864.

[78]*Ibid.*, Statute IV, Chapter XXIV, approved February 6, 1864.

under these acts. Thus Colonel Bayne's Bureau of Foreign Supplies at last had powerful authority under which to function.

Since the government had taken action, even before the passage of the blockade statutes, to assume control of one-third to one-half of the cargo space on private blockade runners, the pattern was laid for regulations to be issued under the new laws. These orders, issued on March 5, 1864, provided that one-half of outbound and inbound cargo space be devoted to Confederate freight at fixed prices.[79]

McRae as agent in charge of disbursements had general supervision of all purchases and contracts in Europe. Acting in that capacity throughout the remainder of the war, he "steadily perfected the purchasing system and Confederate finances." Friction between the European agents vanished under his regime, and the whole fabric of foreign importations tightened up. Cotton was at last put to work in the position which it should have occupied from the start of the war. It was made to serve rather than threaten, to pay rather than bribe. The results achieved by this new cotton concept more than justified the revision.[80]

The Confederacy had in its possession about 400,000 bales of cotton, acquired under the produce-loan statutes, but most of these were in the inaccessible interior. Hence the government had to buy a new supply, located closer to lines of transportation. All the various bureaus went into the field to purchase cotton with which to pay their debts and carry on their operations. Confusion, multiplied and paralyzing, was the result. By August, 1864, however, all cotton buying, east of the Mississippi, was centralized under the Bureau of Foreign Supplies, and the proceeds credited to the Treasury agents in Europe.[81]

A further ramification developed directly out of haphazard departmental cotton purchases. In March, 1864, Charles J. Helm, Confederate agent in Havana, complained of the plethora of autonomous purchasing representatives of various military commands in Cuba. He wanted orders given placing all agents

[79]*OR*, IV, 3, 187–89; Owsley, *King Cotton Diplomacy*, 412–13.
[80]Owsley, *King Cotton Diplomacy*, 409–10, 413.
[81]Owsley, *King Cotton Diplomacy*, 413–14.

there under his direction. Bayne agreed with this idea, and proposed that an order be issued prohibiting the dispatch of special agents to any foreign port to purchase or ship supplies "except in case of most urgent necessity of which necessity report shall be made immediately to the Secretary of War." He also thought the order should forbid trade negotiations in any foreign port where the Confederacy had an agent, except by that official, or on authorization from the Secretary of War. Another exception was to be the commander of the Trans-Mississippi Department, who was allowed to send purchasing agents abroad for his command.[82]

The ships coming in from Bermuda had, in the meantime, been getting ordnance stores to various arsenals in fair quantities. Columbia Arsenal's commanding officer informed Mallet in July, 1864, that 170 bales of cartridge paper, 55 reams of the same for minie ammunition, 1,000,000 pistol caps, 1,250,000 musket caps, 40 bundles copper wire, 230 sheets of sheet brass, 196 sheets of sheet copper, 43 boxes sheet tin, 32 bales serge and 3 cases machine sewing thread, on spools, had been received at the arsenal from Wilmington during June and July.[83]

But the South was never able to count on a steady supply of goods from the islands. In August, 1864, Admiral Farragut, shouting his "Damn the torpedoes," carried the defences of Mobile Bay, and almost completely eliminated that city as a blockade port, though a few runners did get in occasionally.[84] This factor, combined with the general decrease of blockade running, made October a bad month for the Ordnance Bureau. The supply of arms was almost exhausted, and the 17,000 infantry and 7,000 cavalry arms purchased my Major Huse and on the way over, would not meet the emergency, since

[82]Memorandum, Bayne to Seddon, Richmond, April 18, 1864, in Personal File of Thomas L. Bayne, Confederate Records, Adjutant General's Office, National Archives. An indorsement to this memorandum indicates that such an order was issued.

[83]Major J. T. Trezevant to Mallet, Richmond [?], July 25, 1864, in CS Recs., N.A., Chap. IV. vol. 37, 53.

[84]Major General Dabney H. Maury to S. Cooper, Mobile, August 14, 1864, in OR, I, 52, part 2, 723–24.

arsenal production in the Confederacy had fallen off drastically, due to shortages of skilled labor. Gorgas wanted Huse empowered to buy 50,000 arms without delay, in preference to all other purchases. He estimated this would cost about £100,000.[85] Gorgas calculated that due to the loss of ordnance steamers, only 30,000 small arms had been imported east of the Mississippi, and home production accounted for only 20,000, instead of the 50,000 or 60,000 previously anticipated by the Chief of Ordnance. He told Seddon that in addition to the 50,000 Huse was instructed to procure, a like number of arms would be needed for the coming year. Blockade runners too, were still the Confederacy's main source of niter, and lead was becoming more and more necessary.[86] Pressure was being exerted so strongly on blockade runners by the United States Navy, however, that in November Gorgas suggested the sale of some heavy armory machinery awaiting shipment from the islands, since the difficulties involved in bringing in such large equipment were almost insurmountable. Later, a plan was approved to set up an armory abroad in which to use the machinery that could not be gotten to the Confederacy, but the war ended before this idea could be put into effect.[87]

---

[85]Gorgas to Seddon, Richmond, October 5, 1864, Letters Received by the Secretary of War, 1864, document G. W. D. 235, Confederate Records, National Archives.

[86]Report, Gorgas to Seddon, Richmond, October 13, 1864, in *Southern Historical Society Papers*, II, 59–60, and also in *OR*, IV, 3, 733–34.

[87]J. H. Burton to Gorgas, Richmond, February 11, 1865. This letter is in the possession of the daughters of General Gorgas, who reside in Tuscaloosa, Alabama; also, Frank E. Vandiver, "A Sketch of Efforts Abroad to Equip the Confederate Armory at Macon," in *Georgia Historical Quarterly*, XXVIII (1944), 40.

John C. Schwab estimated that during November and December, 1864, about 69,000 rifles came through the blockade. He has obviously confused November, 1864, for the same month of 1863, as Secretary Seddon informed the President that from November 1, 1863, to December 8, 1864, 69,000 arms were brought in. Schwab seems to have been led into error by a statement in Jones's *Rebel War Clerk's Diary*, II, 374–75, quoting the Richmond *Dispatch*. See J. C. Schwab, *The Confederate States of America, 1861–1865*, 239; Seddon to the President, Richmond, December 10, 1864, in *OR*, IV, 3, 930; Diamond, "Imports of the Confederate Government from Europe and Mexico," in *Jour. Southern History*, VI, 477. The mistake

As Sherman's devastating columns pushed through Georgia and Hood's Tennessee campaign thinned Confederate supplies, the blockade assumed even grimmer proportions. Loss of the Ducktown, Tennessee, copper mines by the end of 1864,[88] threw the South's reliance on Europe for its supply of this vital metal. The Ducktown mines had been the source for 90 per cent of the Confederacy's supply.[89]

By March, 1865, both Wilmington and Charleston had fallen into enemy hands, and blockade running shifted base to Havana for the run to Galveston, Texas, and ports on the Gulf coast. Ports in Trans-Mississippi, while perhaps open, afforded no benefit to the armies of Lee and Johnston. These armies had been consuming large quantities of small arms ammunition, and lead was, as usual, precariously short east of the Mississippi. Obviously some available foreign source for arms had to be found when it was considered that from October 25 to December 6, 1864, only 6,560 rifles had entered the South on Government account.[90] In this crisis, Gorgas, and other blockade officials, turned their attention to Florida ports, and less hopefully to Savannah. Some hope was entertained, in March, that supplies might come in through the Union lines. Efforts were afoot to secure some material from that source when the lead shortage in embattled Mobile turned attention to the

is easy to make, due to the ambiguous phrasing of the report of importations. This report, in *OR*, IV, 3, 930, gives total importations from November 1, 1863, to December 8, 1864, but breaks the tabulations into two categories: items received at Wilmington and Charleston "From last statement, Oct. 26, 1864," and those received "From Oct. 26, to December 8, 1864." Hence the obvious error of using October 26 to December 8, 1864, as the inclusive dates of the whole report.

[88]Report of Lt. Col. Richard Morton, Acting Chief of the Niter and Mining Bureau, for period January 1, 1863, to January 1, 1865, in *OR*, IV, 3, 990.

[89]*Ibid.*, and Diamond, "Imports of the Confederate Government from Europe and Mexico," in *Jour. Southern History*, VI, 482.

[90]G. A. Trenholm to the President, Richmond, December 12, 1864, and inclosure, in *OR*, IV, 3, 953–58. The figure in the text is based on the importation of 328 cases of arms, and on the supposition that a "case" of rifles contained twenty arms. See *The Ordnance Manual for the Use of the Officers of the Confederate States Army* (Richmond, 1863), 185.

necessity of removing that City's water mains as the only available source of lead.[91]

While these makeshift measures were being contemplated, military events reached a dramatic final climax. On April 2, 1865, Lee's army evacuated the defences of Richmond and Petersburg and a week later was surrendered at Appomattox Court House. On April 26, Joseph E. Johnston surrendered the Army of Tennessee, followed a month later by General E. Kirby Smith, commanding the Trans-Mississippi Department. Thus ended the Confederacy's hope for victory or negotiated peace, as well as her need for "foreign supplies." Writing long afterward, Major Huse, the indefatigable purchasing agent, said: "When the end came, and some of the largest sellers were ruined, I never heard a word of complaint of their being overreached or in any manner treated unfairly."[92]

Little has so far been said, in this outline, of the supplies secured through Mexico for the Confederate Trans-Mississippi forces. This is not due to oversight, but rather to paucity of material. It is known that vast quantities of stores came from and through Mexico, but the practically autonomous condition of the western department, and absence of its official correspondence files, precludes at this time any comprehensive story of receipts. Efforts of the Cotton Bureau, with headquarters at Shreveport, Louisiana, may be credited with large success in bringing in supplies, but there were numerous other agencies at work, and their records are not available.[93]

----

[91]Gorgas to Mallet, Richmond, March 10, 1865, Personal File of J. W. Mallet, Confederate Records, Adjutant General's Office, National Archives; Lt. James C. Calhoun to Mallet (telegram), Macon, March 15, 1865, in CS Recs., N.A., Chap. IV, vol. 52, 45; Gorgas to Mallet (telegram), Richmond, March 29, 1865, in *ibid.*, vol. 37, 649; Mallet to Gorgas (telegram), Macon, March 28, 1865, in *ibid.*, vol. 52, 49, estimating that, barring enemy interference, 100 to 150 tons of lead would come from Mobile's water pipes. Some lead arrived in Florida in time to forestall taking up the pipes. See Gorgas to Mallet (telegram), Richmond, March 29, 1865, in *ibid.*, vol. 37, 649.

[92]Huse, *The Supplies for the Confederate Army*, 25.

[93]For some material on Mexico to Trans-Mississippi supplies, see Diamond, "Imports of the Confederate Government from Europe and Mexico," in *Jour. Southern History*, VI, 497–502; Owsley, *King Cotton Diplomacy*, 88–145; Thompson, *Confederate Purchasing Operations Abroad*, 103–27; also the Heartman Collection of Confederate Mss, The University of Texas Archives, Austin, Texas.

This general outline, comparatively brief though it is, shows that the Confederacy was almost constantly preoccupied with ways and means to increase the volume of war materials coming through the blockade. Also, it must be apparent that the blockade was, from the Union point of view, far from a completely effective measure. The Federal Navy made strenuous efforts to seal all Confederate ports, but the very magnitude of the task made entire success unattainable.

To say that if the Confederacy had been able to break the blockade it would almost certainly have been able to win the war, or gain a negotiated peace, is too broad. It is, of course, impossible to estimate what unlimited foreign commerce would have meant to the Confederacy. Surely it is not too much to say, however, that the amount of supplies which did arrive through the blockade enabled the Confederate Armies and people to carry on appreciably longer than would otherwise have been possible. It also seems true that McRae's plan was improving with the passage of time, and that if the war had lasted longer, the Confederacy could have gradually built up such a volume of ships trying for the Southern coast that supply shortages would ultimately have been eliminated. The records indicate that blockade running slackened noticeably toward the end, but this was probably due to a growing fear of the South's defeat on the part of blockade brokers, rather than to a breakdown of the organization.

No, blockade running was not one of the Confederacy's blunders. It was perhaps the most successful, large-scale campaign attempted by the South. Its failure was not due to any weakness in its own make-up, but to the collapse of its foundation—the collapse of the Confederacy itself.

The letter-books printed below, comprising Part I of this book, were kept by two different men. All but one of the books were those of John Tory Bourne of St. George's, Bermuda. He acted as Confederate Commercial Agent for Bermuda, and his letters throw considerable light on commercial problems of the Confederacy. The remaining letter-book was kept by Major Smith Stansbury, commander of the St. George's Confederate ordnance depot. His letters are, of course, most important for information on shipments of munitions into the Confederate States.

Some of the Bourne letters follow typed copies in the St. George's Historical Society. The bulk of them, however, follows the original letter press books, in possession of the Hon. William E. S. Zuill, "Orange Grove," Smith's Parish, Bermuda, who kindly consented to write a Prefatory Note to Part I and who graciously gave permission to publish the Bourne and Stansbury letters.

Not all letters in the original books are printed, since many relate to private business transactions and not to blockade affairs. The editor has tried to make a careful selection and present most of those that do deal with the blockade.

Part II of this volume contains cargo manifests of blockade runners which left St. George's, Bermuda, for Southern ports. These manifests were located in St. George's through the kindness of Mr. Hereward Watlington, Mr. Hugh Miller, and Mr. Harry Parker, of Hamilton. The editor hopes that they approximate all the runner's manifests in the Custom House at St. George's.

The letters are printed in their original order, and they are published in different "books" exactly as they were found. This arrangement seems better than printing them chronologically, in view of their extent. The editor has taken the liberty of making minor corrections in the documents, where they seemed necessary for the sake of clarity.

FRANK E. VANDIVER.

Austin, Texas
May 9, 1947

Editor's Acknowledgments

First should come the story of how the cargo manifests of the Confederate blockade runners came to be found, since Mr. Zuill, in his Prefatory note, has explained the finding of the letter books. During the course of a conversation which the editor was having with the Hon. Hereward Watlington in Hamilton, Bermuda, one afternoon in November, 1946, it was remarked that the cargo manifests of these ships would be most interesting if they could be found. Mr. Hugh Miller, who overheard this remark, said that he knew where they were. He had served as Collector of Customs at St. George's, Bermuda, for some time, and during his tenure of office had come across these documents. There had been no systematic or serious effort made to preserve them, and he at once pressed for the construction of a book case, in the Custom House, for their adequate protection. After a time his efforts were successful, and historians are deeply in his debt. Mr. Harry Parker, the present Collector of Customs at St. George's, was most kind and helpful to the editor. Through Mr. Parker's good offices, the manifests were made instantly available, and everything was done to simplify the editor's task.

To the Hon. Hereward Watlington, Hamilton, whose kindness and encouragement will not be forgotten; to the Hon. W. E. S. Zuill of "Orange Grove," Smith's Parish; to Mr. Hugh Miller and Mr. Harry Parker, of Hamilton, the editor tenders his heartfelt thanks. Without their generous assistance, his trip might have come to nought.

The editor also wishes to thank Dr. Eugene C. Barker, Dr. A. P. Brogan, Mr. E. W. Winkler, Dr. Barnes F. Lathrop, and the Research Council of The University of Texas, for their valuable advice and for granting funds to publish these documents. To his grandfather, the late Henry B. Everson, the editor is indebted for encouragement and help.

In conclusion, the editor wishes to acknowledge, with deep appreciation, his indebtedness to The Rockefeller Foundation, for the award of a fellowship which made his trip to Bermuda possible.

FRANK E. VANDIVER.

Austin, Texas
May 9, 1947

Part I

Letter Books of John Tory Bourne
and
Major Smith Stansbury, C.S.A.

Editor's Note to Part I

The Prefatory Note by Mr. W. E. S. Zuill will explain how the Bourne-Stansbury letter-books were discovered. Mr. Zuill, "Orange Grove," Smith's Parish, Bermuda, is the owner of the originals.

John Tory Bourne, commission merchant of St. George's, Bermuda, was the author of four of the five letter-books comprising Part I of this volume. His letters are important for the information they contain on Confederate commercial enterprizes in Bermuda and the blockade business which flourished there. Bourne was Confederate Commercial Agent for Bermuda, and as such was in the best possible position to write of Southern affairs in the islands.

The fifth letter-book in Part I, is that of Major Smith Stansbury, Confederate States Army. Major Stansbury was the Commanding Officer of the Bermuda Confederate Ordnance Depot, and his letters shed much light on efforts to import ordnance into the Confederacy, one of the most important missions of the blockade service.

In editing these documents for publication, the editor omitted many letters which did not bear particularly on the blockade, or which were not of sufficient importance seemingly to warrant inclusion here. Of Bourne's letters, some ninety have been deleted, and some fifty-five of Stansbury's letters have been omitted. Portions of the letters here printed have been left out, since large parts of these letters were of no apparent importance. In most cases a note has been added describing these deletions, and in all cases ellipses indicate omissions.

Bourne Letter Book Number One
August, 1861–December, 1862

12 August 1861

Daniel Draper & Son, Boston.

Gentlemen:—Should any of the ship owners of your City wish British Register I will be happy to assist them here in that. The following documents are necessary: Provisional Register for the time being Power of Attorney with British Consul certificate authorizing the Captain or Person in charge of vessel to sign all papers for the owner. British Consul's certificate of sale of vessel.

St. Georges, Bermuda.
12 September 1861.

Sir:—Having learnt through the columns of the New York Herald and other Journals that the Schooner "Prince Leopold" for whom I obtained a Register from the Comptroller of Customs at the Port of Hamilton in these Islands, had been seized by the Authorities in New York and believing that the information conveyed to them has arisen out of a report which was current here on the arrival of the "PL" to the effect "that Capt. Wallace had run the blockade," I now take the liberty of stating to you the manner in which this property fell into my hands—the facts are as follows:

On the morning of the 9th ultimo I went on board the "Prince Leopold" who had arrived into this Port the evening before, and offered my card to the Captain requesting him to call at my office; after a lapse of two hours Capt. Wallace the master of the "PL" called as I had requested. He opened his business to me by stating that this being the nearest port, he had called in to obtain a British Register, placing into my hands three documents, namely

Provisional Register for the time being, bearing date at Charleston, S.C. 16 July 1861, granted by Mr. Robert Bunch, the British Consul for North Carolina.

Power of Attorney from the owner of the "PL" Mr. Mc-Cleod with Mr. R. Bunch's certificate, bearing date 18th July 1861, authorizing Capt. Wallace to act as his (the owner's) agent here, in obtaining a British Register for the "PL" in compliance with the Mercantile Shipping Act 17 & 18. Victoria Chapter 104 Clause 35 and

A certificate (certified copy herewith enclosed) stating that there was no United States Custom House open by the Government at New Bern and on the date thereof the port of New Bern was NOT blockaded by any of the United States Force.

These documents I placed into the hands of the Comptroller of Customs at the Port of Hamilton on the 9th Ultimo requesting him to grant me a Register for the "PL." He stated that as this was the first case which had come up, he could not grant the Register at first sight, but would refer the documents to His Ex. the Governor, who acts here as Commissioner of Customs; I requested the Surveyor may be ordered to measure the schooner to prevent delay with which he complied; I obtained a certificate of measurement from the Surveyor and on a second application to the comptroller on the 13th ult. to learn the result he informed me that he had received an order from the Commissioner who acted on the advice of the Attorney General to grant me the Register for Prince Leopold which I received; the following morning I cleared her at the Customs House at this port when she sailed for a market.

As agent for the "PL" at this port I take up this business with a view to save trouble to our Authorities in New York and for the benefit of the owner of the vessel and cargo, presuming that Capt. Wallace has made application to you to act in behalf of the owner of this property; I trust the enclosure will enable you to make demand for the immediate release of the "Prince Leopold" and cargo.

I beg to enclose a letter for Capt. Wallace who I learn is held as a prisoner and will thank you to see that it is put into his hands.

John T. Bourne

St. Georges, Bermuda.
12 September 1861

Capt. Geo. Wallace, Schooner "Prince Leopold" New York.

Dear Sir:—This letter will be placed into your hands by Our Consul in New York to whom I have communicated the circumstance of your arrival here, and have enclosed him a copy of the certificate with which Mr. Bunch furnished you in Charleston shewing that the Port of New Bern was NOT blockaded by any of the United States force.

On learning that the "PL" had been seized I immediately called on the Comptroller of Customs at the Port of Hamilton for copies of the documents which you placed into my hands, and which are *now* in *his* office. He stated that I could take copies of the whole if I thought proper, but the certificate of clearance from New Bern was all that would be necessary as it was on that document His Excellency the Governor as Commissioner of Customs ordered him to grant me the Register for the "PL." The enclosure to the Consul—is certified. I could have obtained copies of the whole from the Governor by applying officially which would take time and I should lose this opportunity to communicate with you—presuming that Lord Lyons has written to Mr. Bunch on the subject, should he have received no answer before this arrives, I trust the document enclosed to the Consul will be sufficient for him to make immediate demand for the "Prince Leopold" and her cargo and that Lord Lyons will notify to the Federal Government that for the future more respect is necessary to be shewn to the British Flag. As I feel interested in this business I will thank you to let me know the result.

I cannot close without referring to the occurrence which took place in the Ferry Boat on our return from Hamilton the evening we received the Register, from *whom* I have every reason to believe the information that the "PL" ran the blockade" emanated, it being thence indirectly conveyed to the authorities in New York.

John T. Bourne

St. Georges, Bermuda
30th November 1861.

Keith & McLean, Halifax, Nova Scotia.

Gentlemen:—Your esteemed favours came duly to hand and I have to apologize for the former one being unanswered; the fact was the Confederate War Steamer "Nashville" fell into my hands and being wishful of dispatching her as soon as possible, I was obliged to oversee the labourers coaling day and night—the "Delta" coming in on Sunday and leaving the same afternoon I had no time.

John T. Bourne

Port of St. Georges, Bermuda.
4th January 1862.

A. I. M. Gilbert, Asst-Receiver General St. Georges.

Sir: Having learned from reliable authority that two Vessels laden with coal for the United States War Steamers have arrived into this port and that others are expected to follow up.

I beg leave to state to you that this act of the United States Government in forming a depot for coal at this port or that of Hamilton is highly prejudicial to the Mercantile interest of this Colony and how far it may effect us in a Military point of view I am unable to say.

I therefore trust you will move the proper authorities to consider this case before you permit the landing of the coals in question.

John T. Bourne

[Answer to Above]

Cutom House, St. Georges,
6th January 1862

Sir:—I am instructed by the Governor to acquaint you that he is aware there are at this port certain vessels laden with coal and which he is informed are consigned to the American Consul and that this Gentleman has the same liberty to have coal vessels consigned to him that any other Merchant has.

A. I. M. Gilbert, Asst. Rec. Genl

St. Georges, Bermuda.
22nd January 1862

The Hon. James M. Mason   Confederate States Commissioner
  London

Sir:—I take the liberty of forwarding by this mail to your address (post paid) the History of our little Island by a late reliable author which I trust you will receive safe.

I regret that your visit was very unexpected and our interview so short that you could not avail yourself of judging of the faculties offered at this Port in a business point of view, as a half way house for commerce between the Confederate States of America and the Mother Country.

With reference to the question now at issue I shall continue to tender my services on every occasion which may come up and trust I may be beneficial in furthering the cause. Any business intrusted to my care shall have my personal attention as heretofore.

John T. Bourne

St Georges, 24th March 1862.

Fraser Trenholm & Co. [Liverpool]

Gentlemen:—Referring to my letter of the 6th inst. enclosing disbursements of steamer "Economist" I have now the pleasure of informing you of the safe arrival of the steamer "Bermuda" Capt. Westendorff and "Herald" who has just arrived in port, also steamer "Southwick" from London all well; these vessels are all in my hands and to whom I will give my personal attention in every minute particular; I took Capt. W. to Mr. Butterfield and as time will not permit me to go into further particulars I must refer you to Capt. W. for whom I am and what I have hitherto been doing. The "Ella" has not yet come up. I have just bought 295 tons coal at 35/ for the Herald & Bermuda. I will put the Southwick to sea early in the morning—with apologies for this hurried letter.

John T. Bourne

St. Georges, 27th March 1862

John Fraser & Co.   Charleston, S. C.

Gentlemen:—referring to my letter per Southwick I forgot to say that Tar and Pitch will also fetch a paying price; say 250 bbls each, the Dockyard authorities are in want of it, the last brl of Tar in this market sold for Ten Dollars; steamers returning to Europe may bring on deck pitch pine boards which would pay a freight and port charges.

On my holding a strong letter of recommendation from my friend Lieut Pegram of the C.S.S. of War Nashville connected with other circumstances and on being introduced to Capt. Westendoff his business has fallen into my hands, and which now leads me to believe it will all pass through me as it may arrive, and to whom I refer you for further explanation.

The port of St George as you will observe in the Chart is easy of ingress and egress for steamers and sailing vessels of large class, say drawing 20 feet. Our pilots are very skilful and all natives, the facilities for coaling steam ships are greater than in Madiera, the coal there being carried off in lighters; at this Port I put the ships alongside the wharf, coaling with Barrows, which considerably facilitates their movements and in fifteen minutes after their anchor is weighed the ships are at sea. Labour just at this time is high, namely 5/ per diem, 3/6 & 4/ is the usual rate but there are so many ships arriving here and discharging their cargoes to make repairs the labour is scarce.

The Port of Hamilton is navigable for middle class vessels, drawing 8–12 feet water at ½ tide; the passage is narrow and no ship of the "Bermuda" class was even attempted to be taken in there. Vessels bound for the Port of Hamilton generally pass round St Georges and go a distance of 18 miles before reaching Hamilton and return the same before being at sea. The moorings of all the Man of War are in an open roadstead called Grassy Bay, immediately opposite the Dockyard and when they undergo repairs they are hauled into the Camber which is a kind of Dock built at a very heavy expense by the Admiralty Department.

With regard to the charges made by mercantile men doing business in this Island are as follows: 5% on disbursements of ships paid in cash or bills. 2½% on all goods reshipped. 5% on all articles sold at Private sale or auction. Money loaned 5–10, 15, 20, 25 and even 30% has been charged; the Colonial Law allows legal interest 7%.

Should all this business pass through my hands I propose to charge 2½% on the disbursements of ships coming from you or from Messrs. Fraser Trenholm & Co, Liverpool to my address, and for any sale which I may be requested to effect 5 per cent commission, as from the want of a Bank here, I will have to help it as circumstances turn up. As regards reshipments or transshipments, I consider the charge of 2½% much too high on the business now in hand; I therefore propose that as your risk & that of Messrs Fraser Trenholm & Co with the party concerned are very great, and wishing to use every economy and at the same time furthering the cause at issue, I will defer making any charge for trans shipment of produce either way, but will execute all the Custom House business, writing &c (which will be considerable) and when you close up all the transactions on the acknowledgement of the Confederacy by the European Powers, you will remunerate me as you feel disposed; by this means I risk with all concerned, what my circumstances permit, any loss which may be sustained in transshipment, I also lose a little. At the Custom House in this port I have to Detail myself in the Inward Record Book, every item with marks from manifest, and make inward entries when the cargo (or even a box) is trans shipped. I have to repeat the same in the Outward Record Book, pass Outward Entry and clear vessel for Sea.

I cannot effect the sale of Foreign Bank Bills on any terms, there is no bank in the Island; private Bills if large on England are difficult to negotiate. The Commissariat Department supply our little market with drafts on the Treasury in England at 30 days for ½ percent premium from £50 and upwards as offered for. My offering bills for liquidating the disbursements of steamers arriving here from England and clearing at Customs for the West Indies with Authority opens the business to inquisitive people, therefore it would save considerable trouble for the parties in England to put on board three or four hundred pounds in Gold and insure it, by that means the supercargo with my assistance will be independent; he can put his hands in his pocket and pay down for what he wants at the lowest rate; for instance in the case of the "Economist" I paid down the money for 50 Tons of coal before it was delivered me; after Mr. Butterfield refused to take a draft on Messrs Fraser, Trenholm & Co I took it myself rather than have further detention.

The Liverpool Bank Checks if in small amounts of £25 to £150 would suit this market best, or Messrs F. T. & Co sending vessels to my address with letters of credit for liquidating disbursements. I could then draw as would best suit the purchaser which would be sold at par, and the business be quiet, all parties would be the gainer in the end.

Please say the price which potatoes and onions are likely to fetch in your market about the 1st May.

John T. Bourne

St Georges, Bermuda.
8th April 1862

Fraser, Trenholm & Co   Liverpool

Gentlemen:—I have to inform you of the safe arrival of the Herald Captain Tate on the 24th ult. in 15 days from Madeira; I regret to communicate to you the following facts respecting her.

On the morning after her arrival it came to my knowledge that the whole crew were in a state of mutiny, the Engineers stated to Capt Tate they learnt since their arrival that the ship was bound for Charleston, they would not go, and if on their going to sea they found her steered in that direction, they would stop the engines; on my going on board to look after the delivery of coal I found no discipline and the work progressing very slowly; great dissatisfaction and ill feeling was shewn by Capt Tate towards Mr Mitchell which I do not consider Mr M. deserving of; Capt T. is totally unfit to be in charge of this property and *no nerve* to enable him to persevere with Mr M. to take the ship to her port of destination, this fact became known to the world on the morning of the 28th ult. when Capt Tate with Mr Fraser the 1st Engineer without ever making reference to any one on board or to me as Agent, went to the Mayor's office and noted a protest (certified copy of which Capt Westendorff will enclose you) and put himself under the Federal Consul Mr Allen at this port, who advises him (as Capt T. tells me) by no means to let the vessel go out of port until the owners are heard from. Capt T. gets into a carriage with Mr Allen and goes to see the Governor, a distance of ten miles; his Excellency replied very short, and to this effect "that if he (Capt T.) had any complaint to make it must be in writing"—Capt. T. retained Mr Harvey the Solicitor General; Mr. H. has done all he could to over rule prejudice but says under the mercantile shipping act he cannot be removed from the ship. I took the opinion of Mr. Gray the Attorney General and Lawyer Darrell who stated that the articles of the ship which Capt Tate and crew signed at Liverpool state that "the ship is bound to Bermuda, the West Indies and back to the United Kingdom in 12 months, that there is no legal means of removing Capt T. & crew from said ship till the voyage is performed unless it be by sickness and other casualties." Mr. Mitchell and myself then requested Mr. Darrell to offer compromise to Capt T. I had them all at my office with Mr Smith (who used every means possible) Mr Mitchell retired. Mr. Darrell told Capt Tate that as he did not wish to go to Charleston say what he would relinquish his charge for; he replied that the voyage was for 12 months "and he thought that his wages ought to be paid him for that time." I offered him £50 in Gold with a free passage to England. After considerable discussion he came down to six months wages to clear off with. We then dictated a letter for him to write to the Comptroller of Customs "stating that he (Capt Tate) did not intend to proceed any further in the ship and wished to be discharged here"; he left the office as Mr Darrell and the others supposed to write this letter; instead of which he allows the Consul Allen to take him into Messrs. Higgs & Hyland's office (which I saw myself) where instead of writing the letter as dictated, he writes one to the Governor (who was on the spot at the moment) who in reply tells him that he cannot sanction his leaving the ship. . . .[1]

Capt Westendorff has drawn on you in two drafts in my favour for £110 which please accept.

The Economist has arrived all safe; I enclose copy of a letter to Messrs Fraser & Co for your perusal—trusting all will turn out for the best and your relying on my personal attention & confidence.

John T. Bourne

St Georges,
9th April 1862

Fraser, Trenholm & Co   Liverpool.

Gentlemen:—Referring to my letter of yesterday via St Thomas I have to add that the Mate of the Herald was yesterday sentenced by the Magistrate to be imprisoned till the ship was ready for Sea; finding himself in that position he agreed to take his discharge with wages to date, amounting to Six Pounds, and the further sum of £19 lodged at Custom House for the payment of passage to any port in the United Kingdom; he felt disposed to give further trouble and the Custom House Officer with his consent immediately wrote him off the articles; he has nothing further to do with the ship. The three Engineers left yesterday afternoon for St. Thomas, the remaining portion of the crew seems of two minds, and it does not appear to me from what Mr Mitchell says they are to be relied on or Capt Tate and all Engineers say that the whole affair originated from Capt Tate and all here with myself are of the same opinion; if we succeed in getting her away there will be sufficient reliable persons on board to manage him; at present nothing further can be done as I know of, therefore with a view to get Captain Tate and the remaining portion of the crew out of the ship will be for the Registered Owners of the Herald to send a Power of Attorney to some one here duly authorizing the sale of the Herald (nominally) and orders as to the cargo. I thought first of attaching the

---

[1]Thirty-two lines here omitted recount Bourne's efforts to remove officers and crew from the ship. For results, see letter of April 9, 1862.

vessel for amount of disbursements and selling up and Capt Westendorff to buy her in order to save money and get rid of Capt and crew; my advisers said the Capt would thwart me by saying, sell the cargo and coal and in the absence of charter party, Mr Mitchell has no documents to show that he is supercargo. All this business seems to be left solely into the hands of Capt Tate, a person totally unfit in every capacity to carry out the plans entrusted to him, which I trust for the future will be guarded against. . . .[2]

I presume Capt Carter of the Ella has written you; I put the ship through the Custom House at this port; he called on Mr. Butterfield at Hamilton and is now awaiting orders. The S.S. Southwick left on 25th ult. with fair wind & as nothing has turned up relative to her by the Halifax mail arrived yesterday, which brings American dates to the 4th inst. we may consider her arrived at her port of destination. . . .

John T. Bourne

St. Georges, Bermuda
22nd April 1862

Jno Fraser & Co.   Charleston, S.C.

Gentlemen:—I have this day trans shipped on board the Bermuda, Capt. Westendorff at his request as follows: 120 roles baggage, 146 bags coffee, 217 half chests tea, 180 coils rope, 5 bales twine, which I trust will arrive safe.

John T. Bourne

5th May 1862

Burgess & Stock, London.

Gentlemen: The Southwick having called here for coal on her way to Nassau and having returned here from that place on her way to England in want of the same article and my having on both these occasions transacted the business I now take the liberty of enclosing my card & I will be thankful for any favours which you may confer on me.

---

[2]A paragraph here omitted relates difficulties suffered by passengers on the *Herald*, and mentions funds advanced them by Bourne.

Capt Bird the supercargo brought letters from Messrs Adderly & Co of Nassau to Mr. N. T. Butterfield of the Port of Hamilton and I immediately forwarded Capt B by inland conveyance to Mr. B's office from whom I received a letter authorizing me to supply the ship with what was required, taking Capt Hark's order on him for the amount.

Payment for the supplies, Port Charges &c could have been made me at this port by a draft on you, which would have saved the 5 percent interest, but as the letter was specially to Mr. Butterfield as a matter of courtesy I did not object.

It is necessary that I should explain to you the following; when the Southwick arrived here from England in March last you will observe in my account with the Captain that the coal was charged at 30/ per ton, this coal was the remainder of a lot which belonged to Mr. N. T. Butterfield and the late Mr. E. B. Todd; as Mr. B. was desirous of closing up the transaction with the widow of the latter Gentleman, I obtained it from her at the 30/ and which was all remaining in the hands of any mercantile man in the Island. The Coal now shipped will appear in my accounts at 42/ per ton; by my influence it was placed in my hands for sale; on account of the very high freight (19/ & 22/6) from Cardiff & other incidental expenses has made it tell up considerably over the low rate heretofore charged, as it was ordered to be the best and fresh from the mines to generate steam and not to smoke; the parties to whom I have supplied it going South has never complained of it, and for whom I was induced from Family Ties to use my efforts to prevent delay or other local obstacles. Another cargo will be shipped to my address with the quickest dispatch possible by Henry Bruce Esquire, Bell Court, Mincing Lane to whom I refer you.

John T. Bourne

St Georges, 23 April 1862

Zachariah C. Pearson & Co   London.

Gentlemen:—Enclosed I beg leave to hand you copy of disbursements of steamer Stettin Capt Johnston who arrived into this port in want of coals she left this morning all well for her port of destination.

John T. Bourne

St Georges, Bermuda.
16th May 1862

Fraser, Trenholm & Co.   Liverpool.

Gentlemen:—Your esteemed favour of the 19th ult. came duly to hand with its enclosure. I forwarded Capt Westendorff letter under cover to Messrs Adderly & Co at Nassau before I learnt of his interception; the other letter I received under cover will go by the Ella who will sail tomorrow for Nassau should the wind be fair.

Mr. Heyliger[3] who arrived here in the Gladiator from Nassau on 7th inst. placed in my hands a very kind letter from Messrs Jno Fraser & Co of Charleston dated 16th April wherein they state it is their wish the Ella and Bermuda to proceed to Nassau and refers to availing themselves of my services for the future.

I put Mr Heyliger in possession of the correspondence to you on the Herald; you will read from his letters how the business stands at present.

I received a note from Capt Westendorff dated 7th inst.; I instantly gave it to Mr Heyliger & I requested him to transcribe it to you; it came by a sailing vessel, I got it out of the Post Office; I shewed Mr H the Custom House books and all the transactions of the Bermuda; no doubt Westendorff got his information from a reliable source; speaking of "friends" he means all *Southern Vessels* under British colours bound to Nassau. The fact is the Washington Govt is driven to such desperation at the South burning the produce of the country and retreating that they will do anything; the Bermuda they were determined to have cost what it may, and they have got her; in closing this subject I can only say that all this trouble has arisen out of Capt. Tate and his engineer. . . .[4]

Mr. Dunn and his party leaves in the Ella. He has drawn on you for £122.19.9. Of this sum £2.19.9 is for endorsing bill at 2½% which Mr. Heyliger wished me to charge; its all fair enough between business men & I always do it where I take drafts for disbursements of vessels, but in the case of the

---

[3]Louis Heyliger, Confederate agent at Nassau. See introduction.
[4]One paragraph here omitted, explaining charges for coal.

C.S.Govt it increases their liabilities and all charges should be made as light as possible to make the means go further, I requested Mr H. to explain it.

John T. Bourne.

4th June 1862

Fraser Thenholm & Co.   Liverpool.

Gentlemen:—Your esteemed favour of the 15 & 16 ult came duly to hand yesterday, the latter introducing Mr Wilson; I will take such pleasure in forwarding his views, the contents of the former I note. Immediately on Mr. Wilson's arrival last evening we proceeded on board the Herald with Capt Tate and Mr W. requested him to furnish his acct &c & the papers of the ship; he did not hesitate but seemed disposed to come into Mr. W's terms; Mr W and Mr Heyliger with the Assistant Receiver General are gone to see the Governor (as Commissioner of Customs) and I do not apprehend any difficulty of getting her away in a few days.

In my letter to you of the 16th ult I informed you that I have received a letter from Messrs Jno Fraser & Co state that the Ella was to proceed to Nassau; she left this on the 22nd ult being towed to sea by Govt Tug. Mr Dunn and his party left in her with the Printing Materials and Stationery ex Herald.

I will write you further particulars via Halifax N.S.

John T. Bourne.

June 1862 [No day]

John Fraser & Co.   Charleston, S.C.

Gentlemen:—Your highly esteemed favour of the 16th April was placed into my hands by Mr. L. Heyliger of New Orleans who arrived here from Nassau in the Gladiator on the 7th ultimo.

I assure you sympathy for the South is now being more widely felt and particularly so when their wishes are put before all Christian Men in a truthful light; at this distance we are better able to judge of the progress of the North; they have done nothing; the taking possession of the Sea port towns was expected on account of their superior force by sea; on shore even with assistance of Gun Boats they have been defeated and driven back; no confidence can be placed in any of the Northern Papers, they invariably claim a Victory but their so called Victorious Army never *pursues* always retires— by that means the world judges of their defeat.

There is not the slightest chance for McClellan's army with or without Gun Boats, his quantity of men (if all be true 200,000) are cumbersome on an enemy's soil; the English people are very much cut up over Mr. Russell's not being allowed to go with the Army; they say 'the Federal Govt are afraid that the truth will be known'—the crises is closed on you, so sure as there is a lope hole to New Orleans or any other of the open ports where an ounce of produce can be got at to ship through the Federal Revenue Officers the chance for the South is gone this time; the people of England are pressing the Govt's hand and France feels it keenly; the interception of British Vessels by the Federal cruisers are creating the Trent feeling over again.

I presume you have heard of the capture of the Bermuda;
. . .

In accordance with your wish the Ella left this [port] for Nassau with the Engravers Printers & Some of the materials ex Herald which I trust will all arrive safe with you.

As it appears from the interception of the Bermuda and Circassian, the latter French or a French House (taken 20 miles off Havana) that Westendorff's information has been obtained from a reliable source and the interception of all British vessels is done with a view to prevent supplies reaching the Southern Ports and give the North more time. I would suggest that you divide your business between this port and Nassau; ocean water all round Bermuda outside the reef; the cruisers having no coal within 600 or 700 miles will not be able to hold on for any length of time and any accident occurring to their machinery the Dockyard authority will be very cautious what leniency they give. The Nashville is a good ocean steamer loaded with cargo at Wilmington sufficiently deep to allow her to pass over the Bar and come to Bermuda, coal and water, send more produce and fill her up here, she will go to Liverpool in 17 days, return here with quick dispatch and a full cargo; then the Herald be here to lighten her and both go to you, or let the N. return to England. The Yanky's are constantly on the look out for the Nashville—she can be seen at a very long distance off.

I think now is the time to run as much produce into Bermuda as you can while the course is all clear; sailing vessels also.

So many steamers arriving at Nassau concerned with other parties draws the cruizers on the ground.

The Heralds business has been disastrous to your plans but she is now in a fair way to reach you. I enclose copy of my instructions from F. T. & Co respecting her.

The buildings for warehoused goods at this port are all built of stone consequently fire are unknown. Wooden sheds or buildings are not allowed by the Corporation Law to be erected; the usual manner of warehousing goods are for two months certain or per month as may be agreed on. I hire stores myself which would contain 1 M bales cotton.

I regret to learn the loss of the Gordon; should the Bermuda be given up and come to Bermuda I will suggest to Capt. W. (should he have no orders) to wait here till he hears from you, and should the Herald or any very fast steamer be here I would send the sm. [?] in preference to any other mdze as I presume it must be in constant demand.

Mr. Cameron from Wilmington arrived here on Friday last and has reshipped his little cargo in a vessel for London. He proceeds to Nassau in a day or two.

The steamer Stanely from Liverpool arrived into port this morning; his other friends will follow soon & proceed to Nassau; unfortunately for them they cannot deviate, otherwise their cargo may be in Southern States in less than four weeks. Any business which you may commit to my care shall have my personal attention.

John T. Bourne

P.S. re coal: The last cargo the Economist, Stettin, Southwick, Gladiator & Herald purchased

St. G. 14th June 1862

Fraser, Trenholm & Co., Liverpool.

Gentlemen:—Referring to my letter of the 4th inst. I am now happy to inform you that the Herald left here for Nassau yesterday and it has given me much satisfaction that Mr Wilson met Mr Heyliger to assist in getting her off. It was not necessary to make sale of the vessel as Mr W. will explain to you; we put Mr Mitchell on the register and an excellent mate from the Schooner Jane Campbell, a native of Virginia, the Capt; supercargo, Mate and crew of a small vessel who ran the blockade a week ago are passengers en route for Wilmington. . . .[5]

I am daily expecting the cargo of coal from Cardiff which was ordered by the Economist and a further supply of Cumberland from Baltimore. Mr Wilson[6] has written you to ship 500 Tons, I would suggest 1 M, because I may have the chance of supplying a large lot to a Spanish or French vessel bound north, at any rate I should have a reserve stock of 300 to 500 Tons to meet any failure which may occur to any of your vessels who may not succeed in getting through the Blockade or from Nassau bound home.

The Federal Cruizers having instructions to intercept all steamers bound to Nassau, I have suggested to Messrs Jno Frazer & Co per Herald that they divide their business between that port and this, the Cruizers can go to Key West, coal and return to the Bahama Channel in 48 hours, where they can anchor at pleasure, but they cannot do that in these waters, distant 700 to 800 miles from any coal depot—ocean water outside the reef all round Bermuda, they cannot hold on, any accident happening to their machinery the Dock Yard authorities will be very cautious what leniency they give them. Several parties have sent steamers and other vessels to Nassau & I learn that port is full of vessels of all sorts concerned in this trade, which makes it appear dangerous. We have not had a visit from any of them.

---

[5]One paragraph concerning coal is here omitted.
[6]James A. Ker Wilson, of the firm of Cunard, Wilson, & Co., Liverpool.

The Warehouses here are all built of stone, dry and well ventilated, no wooden sheds or buildings are allowed to be erected by the Corporation Law; therefore fires are unknown. Mr Wilson will give you further local information.

I regret to inform you of the following captures, viz: British Steamers Stettin, Cambria, Patros, Elizabeth and the Nelly was driven on shore all off Charleston. I learn from the master of a Bermuda Vessel who arrived here yesterday, the Federal army suffered severely before Richmond & the papers have said nothing of it.

John T. Bourne

St. Georges, Bermuda, 28th June 1862

Lomnitz & Co   Manchester.

Gentlemen:—By this mail via St Thomas W. I. you will receive my acct current with Mr Ernest Zachrisson, super-cargo steamer Stanley, Capt Haste, for fuel and port charges. The Stanely left this morning for Nassau and having procured her a mail from the Post Master General of this Island I trust she will arrive safe and in good time.

Having been sometime doing business in this General Commission line, I take the liberty of enclosing my cards. Since the Civil War in the States has been going on, my attention has been entirely given to any business bearing a Southern tinge both private and otherwise and will be happy to forward your views or that of your friends at Liverpool when confided to me.

Nassau at this time has become a prominent port for the deposits of British Mdse which I learn is on the increase; Bermuda has not as yet received any appellation from the Federal Powers situated 650 miles from the Confederate States, Ocean water all round outside the reef, a fine harbour affording every facility for coaling &c the Federal Cruizers would not be able to hold on for any length of time and the constant strength of our Navy being always ready for sea, any interruption would be remedied in a few hours.

Unfortunately the Stanley arrived a few days after I closed up my last coal which has caused the great detention, I am momently expecting a further supply and will be able to furnish any steamers who may come up. . . .

John T. Bourne

St Georges, 10 July 1862

Robert Dunlop Esq.

Sir:—. . . The steamer Memphis arrived safe in Charleston, the Columbia left here yesterday; I trust she will succeed; she came to Mr Fisher, the Memphis belongs to the same owners.

John T. Bourne

St Georges, 10 July 1862

Leech, Harrison & Forwood, Liverpool.

Gentlemen:—The steamer Adela, Capt Walker, left this on the 3rd inst. for Nassau, on the eve of his departure and under instruction from you he placed into warehouse under my care 45 cases of Mdze with a letter, copy of which I enclose. On application to Capt Leslie of the Columbia the day before he was ready for sea he told me that time would not permit him to receive them as the fuel he was taking in was all on deck and his men too busy, this I regret; favourable news suddenly arrived which he was obliged to act upon immediately and I trust he will succeed. The steamer Memphis from Nassau arrived safe into Charleston. . . .

Bermuda for the present is better situated for the reception of Mdze en route to the States, we are not particular favourites of the Am Cruizers.

Since the struggle of the C.S. of America for their independence my business has been principally in that way—personal attention being essential to ensure success—any business of a private or other nature I will be most happy to forward, referring you in Liverpool to Mr James A Ker Wilson of the firm of Cunard, Wilson & Co for which gentleman I transacted important business.

John T. Bourne

St Georges 11 July 1862

Fraser, Trenholm & Co.   Liverpool.

Gentlemen:—. . . Nothing has transpired of importance. The Memphis has arrived into Charleston, the Columbia left this yesterday and the Lodona will leave tomorrow for Nassau. The Southern Arms has been successful and I trust will continue.

John T. Bourne

St Georges 14th July 1862

Jesse Jones Esq. Somerset. Of the firm of Smith, Jones & Co. New York.

Sir:—On the 29th ult the steamer Lodona of and from Hull, England arrived into this port in want of fuel; after some conversation with Capt Luckie and the supercargo Mr. Charles Purdue it was arranged that on the next morning I was to put the ship through the Customs. On Capt Luckie and Mr Purdue coming on shore as promised I put the ship through the Customs when Mr Purdue stated that he had about 25 Tons saltpetre, 100 bbls drugs which he wished to trans ship to New York in the first vessel; I stated to him that one vessel was ready for sea, the Hound and that Penguin would be the next; he made a final arrangement with me to ship the Mdze. . . .

John T. Bourne.

St Georges Bermuda 12 July 1862

Jno B. Tatem Esq.   Asst Receiver General

Sir:—Having been informed by you that the saltpetre and drugs which I am about to put on board the Brigantine Princess Royal ex steamer Lodona must not be removed for the present.

I beg to state that this unlooked for detention is prejudicial to the owners of both vessels, and as the articles in my entries are mdze of the same description as shipped from the United Kingdom to open ports in the states of America, and in the absence of any local law to prohibit the exportation of any description of mdze to a friendly port fairly open for trade,

I contend as a man of business that the obstacle is unnecessary as the Lodona will be ready for sea at 12 o'clock today.

John T. Bourne

St George, 10 July 1862

Ashbridge & Co.   Liverpool.

Gentlemen:—Learning from my friend Mr E. Zacherson that you are connected with the Confederate States of America, who are at this moment struggling not without hope in the Allwise disposer of events for Independence, I take the liberty of enclosing my cards and will be happy to assist you or any of your *own friends* through this port with any business of either a private nature or otherwise as may turn up. Since the commencement of the struggle the business which has passed through this port has been committed to my care it being of such nature as to require my personal attention, the parties for whom I have acted, have duly appreciated my motives. With a view that no delay may occur I influenced a friend to assist in establishing a Coal Depot at this port, which from its easy ingress and egress for steamers and sailing vessels of large class to the Oceans with every facility for quick despatch; I was confident that I could give some little assistance in furthering supplies to the South; I therefore in April last held over 1 M Tons coal but from the unprecedented demand on me and the very long passage of the supply from Cardiff to arrive has at this moment left me bare, consequently Mr Z. in the Stanley could only obtain 7 Tons Coal & took wood; the Adela, Columbia & Lodona also took wood, but with a view to the future to prevent this unforseen obstacle I will have on hand a reserve of Sidney or Pictou N.S. coal, which will answer in case of emergency.

Isolated as Bermuda is from the rest of the busy world an outlay of 2 or 3 M Tons of coal in this climate is considerable risk to incur there being no steam communication except with Halifax once a month; this is done by Cunards in conveying the North B Mail through the St Thomas and back to Halifax, consequently the sale is doubtful; the Govt authorities here in all cases promptly responded to all applications from the

Mercantile community for supplying coal, until this struggle commenced and having been necessitated to make repeated application on behalf of the Stanley I have now to enclose you copy of the correspondence on that subject which will not be uninteresting to you. Being suspicious should they supply one steamer they must the whole (if more in market) which would so reduce their stock as would be detrimental to the interest of the service, everything here (at present) being on a war footing.

Bermuda is situated on the direct line from Charleston to Liverpool that it struck me on the acknowledgement of the Independence of Confederate States by the European Powers that a line of steamers from that port or New Orleans touching here for coal may be in contemplation, and if such be the anticipated arrangement I would be able to supply the necessary fuel on moderate terms; presuming the steamer would be large class the passengers money would probably pay all expenses at this Port and no doubt the Legislature would place such line of steamers on the same footing as they did the Royal W.I.M. [West India Mail] Packets, when they touched at Bermuda.

Nassau being the rendezvous for so many steamers, I fear the Federal Cruizers will greatly interfere with arrangements made in England; I think that if this business was a little divided between that port and this a better chance may be afforded in bringing supplies from England without molestation; with reference to the contents of steamers cargoes arriving here, the articles of Gunpowder *cannot* be removed from the ship as there is no magazine to put it in; all the Govt magazines are over full and the authorities in England have been requested not to send any more there being no store rooms for its reception; other merchandise can be stored at reasonable rates, as there are large, dry, well ventilated warehouses, all built of stone, no wooden buildings are allowed to be erected, consequently fire is unknown.

I enclose Mr Zachrisson's note to your senior referring you to J. A. Ker Wilson Esq of Liverpool for whom I transacted some business of importance.

John T. Bourne.

11 December 1862

Messrs John Fraser & Co   Charleston.

Gentlemen:—This I trust will be safely handed to you by our Consul, Robert Bunch Esq. under cover to whom I have taken the liberty to put it. I have to inform you that Capt Lockwood left this for Liverpool on the 28th ult in the Stmr Delta via Halifax. He took the opportunity of examining the Merrimac but tells me that she will not answer the purpose and that he will not recommend her to the Liverpool house for purchase, being much too slight. The Phoebe returns to England in a week or two, Messrs Overed Gurney & Co. having taken her to close accts.

I am happy to learn that Coxetter and the Leopard are both safe at Nassau but I regret that Capt Parke and his passengers should have misrepresented our blockade; the facts are that Wilkes was sent here to look out for "290"; after arriving he found the Minho, Ouchette and Merrimac all here at work; after playing his tricks he left for Key West leaving the gun boats Sonoma and Tioga to watch the Minho &c when they were ready. The O. left on Wednesday, Capt Parke on Saturday night and the Gun boats the following night (Sunday) for Havana; so ended our blockade; the report of 10 more being expected was simply set about by the Yankees which Capt Parke and others took in, but on a moments reflection it would have been found that the Yankees had no more to send, all their Gun Boats were employed at Fortress Monroe and your Blockade.[7] We are clear and the only visitors we have had was the San Jacinto, Mohican and Vanderbilt which stayed the usual time one after the other.

The Justitia and Cornubia arrived here from London on 3rd Capt. Styles was passenger, the C. is very fast ship (18) and will be on the wing early next week. Say to the Capt of the Giraffe to look out for his friends and if the Capt of the G. is not where the Kate *was* when you intended to send her

---

[7]Commander Charles Wilkes, U. S. Navy, was sent to watch Bermuda waters for the appearance of the Confederate War Steamer *290*, or *Alabama*. For a time he blockaded the port of St. George's, but did not maintain his position.

to Bermuda, say to the persons *there* to be earlier than usual to business. If Mr Bringlow or one of his capabilities could be there I apprehend no failure, and he would naturally assist the business through, which would be satisfactory to all parties.

I send Mr Bunch Wilmer & Smith—European Times also a Bermuda paper of the 9th inst. Capt. Burroughs exchanged and will be via [illegible] with you Thursday or Friday next all being well.

The papers sent Mr Bunch I actually intend for you and I suppose he will give them to you. Cotton in England has fallen considerably and the distress is said to be dreadful; Capt Burroughs will communicate all the news of importance; our dates are to 15th ult from England & 2nd from New York.

John T. Bourne.

St Georges, 11 December 1862

Jno. Fraser & Co.   Charleston.

Gentlemen:—In accordance with your instruction to Capt Coxetter & on the recommendation of Capt Gage I have purchased the schooner St George of the burden of 103 Tons & when loaded will draw 8–9 feet water. Accounts showing cost and what was actually necessary for the voyage I herewith enclose, also Power of Attorney authorizing Capt Gage to sell the schooner to Mr Lafitte and yourself. Capt Gage left this for Turk's Island on the——ult and I gave him 1,000 sacks; she will have between 4 & 5 M bush. salt and is a fair sailor. You will please find also enclosed the expense of shipping of the 646 bales cotton per Ella who left this last Friday for Liverpool. I kept her till Capt Lockwood arrived from Nassau & as he told me that Capt Parke had misrepresented our Blockade of course I thought it useless to keep her any longer. Capt Parke and his passengers were very much alarmed at the sight of Wilkes & his two gun boats but as I have before said they were after 290 and then Wilkes set them to watch Parke and when he cleared out they went the next night.

The Justitia arrived from England on the 3rd inst. Capt Styles is on board and takes in the Cornubia; the cargo of the Justitia consists of blankets, boots & shoes, medicines and what the South are actually in want of. I would run this cargo in as soon as possible. I shall warehouse it for exportation as soon as the Cornubia is gone. I do not think it prudent to hire ships to bring cargoes to this port and let them lie in the harbour and dip out of them every now and then; it creates suspicion & the storage is nothing compared with the convenience of getting them through. The Harriet Pinckney has been lying in the harbour since August last with arms and a Field Battery and no orders from Richmond. The remains of the Gladiator cargo belonging to you are 566 bbls gunpowder, 500 bags saltpetre. The Justitias cargo I intend putting in the same warehouse upstairs to be ready at a moments warning but there is nothing in the cargo shipped by F. T. & Co for Liverpool. I have arranged the depot business that the ship can coal, land and take in her cargo & water &c, all at same time. You will see by the papers that the Cornubia is very fast and Capt Styles has bought her for the C. Govt, but I scarcely think she will answer for a Gun Boat; perhaps you may be able to induce them to sell her; the boilers are new and all is in prime condition.

John T. Bourne.

26th December 1862

Edward Coleman Esquire, Present.

Dear Sir:—I have to acknowledge the receipt of your letter of the 24th inst. with invoice, also Power of Attorney authorizing me to get for you in certain goods warehoused & now lying in the Islands of Bermuda and in reply thereto beg to say that due attention will be given to the instructions therein contained.

With reference to the Gunpowder warehoused at Tuckers town I consider that as circumstances have now arisen I hold this powder liable for the monies advanced Messrs Z. C. Pearson & Co's ships who have passed through Bermuda some time since & that on the 9th August when you endorsed the Bill of Lading for this powder to me you were acting as the Atty of Messrs Z. C. Pearson & Co, all of which I presume you understand.

John T. Bourne.

Bourne Letter Book Number Two
December, 1862–November, 1863

10 cruisers referred [?] was a report set on foot by the Yankees here to alarm Capt. Parke of the "Minho" and his freighters; nevertheless, masters of steamers must be careful in approaching Bermuda as they would Nassau but if there were cruisers off Bermuda, there is plenty of ocean room to run for it, but at Nassau the cruisers lie in the Channel and steamers must either be captured or run on shore.

Please let me know on whom I am to draw for the storage and rest of the expenses of this cargo when it is all gone; the storage will not be of importance taking into consideration the facilities we now have of sending it. I told Capt. Stiles that the keeping of steamers waiting in the harbour with CS goods caused great suspicion and damage was very heavy, therefore by warehousing for exportation the cargo was out of view and the ships gone, if cruisers came up they could see nothing and those on the look out here (one or two persons) knew nothing to tell and when the steamers from the South came they were disposed of in three or four days without trouble.

John T. Bourne[1]

St. George's, Bermuda
15th December, 1862.

M. B. Lafitte Esquire, Nassau.

Dear Sir:—. . . The "Cornubia" left this for W [Wilmington?] on Saturday last with 520 bales &c. ex. "Justitia" but I fear for want of a pilot she will be with you ere this reaches you. I wrote to C. last week per H.M.S. M. under cover to Mr. B. requesting Messrs. T. & Co. to look out at W. for the C. and the "Giraffe" the latter would coal at Madeira and go across believing when he left Engld. that Bermuda was blockaded.

---

[1]Page 1 of the original of this letter is missing. Exact date and addressee are unknown.

I, this morning, received letters from Liverpool by mail dates
to 29th ultos. with enclosures for Charleston; they say we
do not desire to purchase the "Merrimac" and also approve of
what I have done relative to the "Gladiator's" and "Herald."

John T. Bourne

St. George's, Bermuda
6th December, 1862.

L. Heyliger, Esquire, Nassau.

Dear Sir:—By the mail arrived today from England I have
received a letter from Major Caleb Huse in reply to mine of
30th Oct. last. He says 'I note your remark concerning the
"Harriet Pinckney" that it would have been better to land
her cargo, as the affair has turned out it would have been.
I hope that orders concerning her have been received from the
Coast before this. In case however such should *not* be the case
you will please act in the matter as follows:—

If a pilot can be obtained and the pilot and Capt. agree
that it is prudent to attempt to run in, you will please direct
the Captain to proceed.—As regards compensation to the
Officers, Engineers, etc: You will please inform the Captain
that they will all receive the same pay that is given by John
Frazer & Co. to their Captains and Officers.

If a pilot cannot be secured or if it should be considered
imprudent to make the attempt, you will please receive the
cargo of the H. P. [Harriet Pinckney] and forward it by the
H. P. to London. If freights can be obtained for her to Liverpool, you will, in that case, make all arrangements necessary
in the case and dispatch her to that port. In case, however,
the "Justitia" is ordered to Nassau you will please also order
the H. P. to the same port to discharge. I hope that the Captain of the H. P. and yourself will cooperate with each other
cordially. I have not had any=communication with the Captain of the H. P. I will not complicate matters any more than
they have been already by writing to him.'

C. H[use].

I cannot obtain a pilot here, therefore I would suggest that
you send two or three on their speculation. The Captain of

the H. P. "Halpen" is willing to go under the terms named in Major H.'s [Huse's] letter.

I shall wait till the new moon is half full before I do anything with the H. P. as by that time the "Cornubia" will have returned from the Coast and other arrivals from that way come up. I may have some orders respecting her. If not, I shall warehouse the cargo for exportation—so far as I can see today I do not consider it prudent to send her to the Coast or Nassau, both places being as much blockaded as the other. I have this day entered the cargo of the "Justitia" for exportation and warehousing it in the stores of Mr. Penno, having the balance of the "Gladiator's" there also. This cargo is at this time everything to the U.S.G[overnment]. and I trust that it will shortly be run in, Capt. Stiles formerly Consul at Vienna was [illegible] and requested I would as I have done and [which?] he has acquainted Major H. the "Cornubia" took 500 odd bales blankets, boots and medicines. . . .

John T. Bourne.

St. George's, Bermuda,
16th December, 1862.

Fraser, Trenholm & Co.   Liverpool.

Gentlemen:—Your favor of the 29th ultimo came duly to hand this day with letter for Charleston which I will forward as directed.

The Invoice of Mdse. purchased I will forward you copy of, but the original bills I send with it to Charleston, but I suppose I can get duplicates, I thought I put a copy in with the other documents.

As regards the charge of 5% I got nothing off that, Mr. Black got that benefit, and I told you in my letter that Coxetter asked for more than he actually wanted, but for the future I will show them your letters.

Owing to the report as I said before of Capt. Parke and his passengers relative to our blockade in Charleston appears as Capt. Lockwood says to [have] prevented the Herald and Leopard com.g. to Bermuda.

John T. Bourne.

St. George's, Bermuda
1st January, 1862 [1863].
Per Sch. "Evelina."

John B. Lafitte Esq.   Nassau

Dear Sir:—. . .[2] You will please find enclosed two schedules No. 1 shewg the manner in which the "Gladiator's" cargo stands which belongs to the House. No. 2 shows what belongs to C.S.G. which I trust will be satisfactory. The cargo of the "Justitia" is all warehoused; it consists of Medicines, Blankets, Boots, Shoes, Clothing, value £93,000. which at the time is of the greatest importance to the C.G. The "Harriet Pinckney" is now discharging. You will see in our Gazette the proclamation prohibiting the exporting of Arms etc., but carefully read it and you will see that it's simply notifying that such law has received the sanction [but will not be?] acted on without England is at war with some power. The "Merrimac" was examined by Capt. Lockwood. He told me that he could not recommend her to the House. I will be glad to learn if you have heard anything of the "St. George." Capt. Hora of the "Gladiator" wrote a letter here to some one dated 26th ultimo. He says, "I will leave in a day or two for Nassau." The Str. "Justitia" will leave for England with a few old Govt. stores and ballast early next week.

I send you under cover to Adderley & Co. some newspapers, the Yankee Army under Burnsides [Ambrose E. Burnside] has been destroyed, a gentleman from New York arrived yesterday, stated that the army was nearly annihilated, Stonewall Jackson refused to allow them to bury their dead until they were finally done fighting. Burnside, Seward and Chase have tendered their resignations, but the President will not accept them, Jackson's army has not suffered much being entrenched, other passengers state that it was the most horrible massacre on record; so much for the Enfield Rifle. Federal Jackson with some other Generals are killed. The strs. in harbour are the "Justitia," "H. Pinckney," "Phebe," "Merrimac." . . .

John T. Bourne.

---

[2]Several paragraphs here omitted recite Bourne's agreement to charge 1¼ per cent "on all goods passing through my hands."

St. George's, 2nd January, 1863.

N. T. Butterfield Esquire, Hamilton.

Dear Sir:—Having been informed by Mr. Francis Chambers, Atty. Messrs. Overed Guerney & Co. of London that you were authorized to advance the sum of £500. to assist in defraying the disbursements of Str. "Merrimac," four hundred pounds of which has been paid me on account of that ship, and on my making application to Mr. Chambers requesting him to defray the expense incurred on Str. "Phebe" who I learn from him has been sold, he tells me that you are to make the necessary advance on said ship. Would you be kind enough to do me the favor to say if you are in possession of any authority by general letter of credit from Messrs. Overed Guerney & Co. to make the necessary advance and if so, is it your intention to do it, and on what day will you be prepared to close up? Please let me know by return of mail.

John T. Bourne.

St. George's, Bermuda
1st January, 1863.

Major Caleb Huse, C.S. Army, London.

Dear Sir:—Referring to my last letter I have now to inform you of the arrival of Captain Porter from Nassau on 25th ultimo with precisely the same instructions to land the H.P. [Harriet Pinckney] cargo and send her back to England. Should you not have made a final purchase of the H.P. I would suggest that as it is impracticable to carry ships of the H.P. class through the blockade, not to buy as they will be cumbersome, buy freighting steamers to bring goods, as soon as the goods are landed the ship be given up and you have no trouble with Captains or Engineers etc. When you send any more goods here please have the bills of lading endorsed 'deliver to S. G. Porter or in absence to John T. Bourne' or have them consigned to me and B.L. filled up in my name by that means I can get hold of them at once without trouble, but the bills of lading so endorsed you must send by regular mail via Halifax, giving the Captain a blank copy for himself if he should require it.

I enclose copy of letter from Messrs. John Frazer & Co.
I sent the C. S. goods in without charge, requesting them to
collect from the Gov. what was fair. Capt. Porter communicated my views to the authorities in Richmond and under
these circumstances to charge the 1¼ per cent as therein
stated, and request Messrs. Frazer Trenholm & Co. to settle
it with you as I send home the bills for what goes forward
by this means it will be satisfactory to all but as this is half
the usual charge at this port, I would not like it to be known,
as it may effect other mercantile men who are dependent on
commission business with their families for a living. Mr.
Porter tells me that he has written to you to the same effect.
I therefore enclose bill for what has gone, copy of which I
send to F. T. & Co. for collection. . . .

John T. Bourne.

St. George's, Bermuda,
7th January, 1863.

Major Caleb Huse, C. S. A. Dept., London.

Dear Sir:—This will reach you per Str. "Justitia," Capt.
Holmes, who has safely landed her cargo at this port. We
have had no visits from the Yankee cruisers and are not likely
to have any, the Admiral and fleet have returned from Nassau and will winter at Dk. Yard. You will read in the Rl.
[Royal] Gazette of this Island a proclamation prohibiting the
exportation of Arms and ammunition but as no law of this
kind has ever been sanctioned by the Home Authorities it was
necessary to make it known by proclamation, but it is only
intended for the Governor and Council to act on in case of
hostilities with England, and I learnt to my satisfaction that
it will not effect the cause at issue, so far as I am concerned.

I will write you by regular mail relative to the "Justitia"
if she is entitled to demurrage, also Mr. Begbie.

I have dates from Nassau to 19th ultimo the "Giraffe" had
arrived and would leave in a day or two for the States.

The "Herald" arrived into Charleston on the 17th ulto from
Nassau and the Am. papers say that a fine str. with Blankets
and Shoes arrived in a Confed. Port on 19th, this answers for
the "Cornubia" and it's very likely.

The H. Pinckney will be unloaded about the middle of coming week, by that I am in hopes we will receive a cargo of cotton.

John T. Bourne.

St. George's, Bermuda
7th January, 1863.

Fraser Trenholm & Co., Liverpool.

Gentlemen:—Without any of your favors to refer to, I have to enclose copy of letters received by Capt. Porter from Mr. John Frazer & Co. wherein they suggest that I send you bills for C.S. property to collect as I send it forward. In my letters to them I requested they should call on the Govt. after the goods were delivered; Mr. Porter tells me he named it at Richmond and they referred him to Mr. Trenholm who has settled the manner in which I am to be paid. I shall therefore for the future send the bills forward to you for collection. The 1¼ per cent named is just half the usual charge made at this port by mercantile men so far back as the year 1800 but as it seems satisfactory I have no objection to please all parties and the House has been kind enough to arrange this for me. I shall only make you the same charge, namely 1¼ per cent on all mdse. passing through my hands for the future which I trust will be satisfactory. I have enclosed Major Huse copy of J. F. & Co. letter dated [?] ultimo, also account.

You will see in the copy of the Gazette I send you a proclamation prohibiting the exportation of Arms and Ammunition, this law is framed on the Act of Parliament giving the Governor and Council power in the event of hostilities with England to put it in force immediately the same as in England, so therefore it was necessary that it should be made known—by proclamation was thought best, fearful it may be read in another way I mention it. I saw the Atty. G. personally on the subject and I find it will not interfere with my business or the cause at issue.

I received letters from Mr. Lafitte to 17th ultimo and dates to 19th—"Giraffe" had arrived.

We have not had any visits from the Yankee cruisers of late and we do not expect any, our Admiral has arrived from

Nassau and has taken up his usual winter quarters at the Dk. Yard—I have not heard anything of the arrival of the "Gladiator" at Nassau—The "Justitia" has landed her cargo, and the H. Pinckny is now doing the same. I am in hopes to see Coxetter next week with cotton for the H.P.—The strs. in port are H.P., "Merrimac," Phebe."

John T. Bourne.

St. George's, Bermuda
15th January, 1863.

Overed Guerney & Co., London.

Gentlemen:—Mr. Frances Chambers, your attorney, informed on 13th inst. that he had recd. letters from you stating that the steamer "Phebe" had been sold to the Australia St. Pkt. Company and that Captain Speard had been sent to take charge of her, on my asking Mr. Chambers if he was prepared to pay up the disbursements of the "Phebe" he informed me that no funds had arrived, but that by the coming mail due here on 10th proximo, the necessary funds will arrive; I, this morning, requested Mr. Chambers to let me know what prospect he had to hold out to me that Capt. Johns (the Master) would be placed in funds on the arrival of before-mentioned mail, he said it was probable, I asked him if he had written for funds and he said, No. I told him I was very much surprised as he has let me to believe for the past three months that he had done so; I said nothing more.—

You are aware that the str. "Phebe" and "Merrimac" came into this port as the property of Zc. Pearson & Co. and have incurred considerable expense, the "Merrimac" I have closed up with as follows: £400. cash received from Mr. Butterfield order Mr. Chambers, 989 cases Brandy ex. ship, sufficient to close account, at 20/—per case and the balance of Brandy on account of "Phebe's" disbursement leaving now due thereon about £600 and wages due Captain and Seamen amount to £700. The seamen are very uneasy and desirous of putting the ship in the Court of Vice Admiralty which they can do as Pearsons are bankrupt, and there is some difficulty to prevent, I assured them that they would be paid in full.——

Please act immediately by sending Mr. Chambers a letter of credit on Mr. Butterfield which will enable him to carry out your sale amicably, otherwise the "Phebe" will be in the Court of Admiralty for six months and incur additional expense of £1,000 and delay which will affect your sale.

Hoping you will see the emergency and refer you in London to Hy. Bruce Esq., Hy. Frazer Todd, Thos. Begbie Esq and at Liverpool, Thomas [James?] A. Ker Wilson Esq., from Messrs. Cunard, Wilson & Co., Frazer Trenholm & Co.

John T. Bourne.

P.S. The Brandy I have disposed of which you must deduct from sale of "Merrimac." J.T.B.

St. George's, Bermuda
10th February, 1863.

Major Caleb Huse, C.S.A., London. *Via St. Thomas*

Dear Sir:—Your favor of 7th ultimo per "Miriam" came duly to hand on 30th ultimo and contents noted. I have given Mr. Frances Chambers the receipts for ship and cargo as you will observe by bills of lading which he now holds.—The Brandy referred to in my letter of 24th ultimo Mr. Chambers has supplied me with 1,000 cases which were landed ex. "Phebe" being on examination of same quality, and on his arrival in England will offer you 757 other cases of Brandy being now in my store; but I would suggest to you in buying this Brandy you will not pay for it until you get my receipt or Mr. Walker's in hand as it may turn out troubles me to get at but please keep this to yourself. The "Miriam" is discharging cargo and will leave for Nassau during the coming week.—Mr. Porter is on board the "Merrimac" and we will get her off as soon as the crew can arrive.—

Mr. Walker has conferred with me relative to his position here and with Mr. Porter we all work together without trouble.—The Har. Pinkney's disbursement I will draw for on Mr. Begbie as I forwarded them before Mr. W. arrived. The saving to the CS. Govt. will be considerable if quick steamers can be purchased to run in the goods and bring me cotton for reshipment; one trip in and out will very nearly cover ship and all expenses, the "Cornubia" only brought 300 bales, no more could be got at but she could have carried more. Should the war be prolonged after the closing of Parliament, quick and light draft steamers may be bought on the Lakes in Canada which will answer during the summer months, particularly about Mobile and no doubt at low rates.—

Mr. Chambers will also offer you on behalf of Overed Guerney & Co. 1500 bbls. Gunpowder, Guns, Shells and Claret, but do not (as I did before) pay until you see my receipt or Mr. W. as Messrs. Smith Bros. & Co. of Hull intend entering an action for recovery of this property on bills lading endorsed to them by Zc. Pearson & Co. and which suit is shortly to come off here.—Since Mr. Chambers left I have been served with warning by Smith Bros. & Co., attorney not to move the goods in question, but the said goods are in the possession of Guerney's attorney, Mr. J. W. Musson, if you buy this property on the spot with you, I may not be able to get hold of it. But it will be better for you to know that the dispute is settled between Smith Bros. & Co. and Overed Guerney & Co. before you have anything to do with it.

Your favor, 24th Jan., is also duly at hand; the "Dashing Wave" has not' yet arrived, Mr. Porter and myself received no invoices as you stated, and none of the "Miriam's" cargo either.—Bills of lading are all I have received with nett amt. cargo per D.W. from Messrs. I. Campbell & Co.—

The "Cornubia" has arrived and will leave for Wilmington on Wednesday next.

John T. Bourne.

St. George's, Bermuda
22nd March, 1863.

Fraser, Trenholm & Co., Liverpool.

Gentlemen:—Your esteemed favor of 20th ultimo came duly to hand and contents noted.—

I have to acknowledge the receipt of the £500 through Messrs. Cunard & Co. for which I have to thank you.

I placed into Major Walker's hands your letter enclosed to me.—

I have to thank you for the statement of cost "Gladiator's" cargo, but Messrs. John Frazer & Co. have paid me for that portion which I sent them by the "Herald," and when I send the balance I will charge it at that rate (1¼ per cent), therefore, I need not draw on you for the amount named £265.2/10 as it is not due me.—

With reference to the Cotton, the H.P. [Harriet Pinckney] had in 300 bales which arrived in the "Cornubia" from Wilmington, this Cotton was in charge of Capt. Styles, who consigned it to me with written request that I should consign it to Major Huse by B.L. in London, which I did and at the same time authorizing me to reimburse myself by drafts on Messrs. S. Isaac Campbell & Co. of London. I remarked at the moment that London was no place to send cotton that the proper business manner of work was to attach draft to B.L. as security, forward it in that way, but he did not seem to like it. I therefore to have no contention forwarded loose I took drafts as requested.—

I shall for the future if not paid by Major Walker do as you suggest.—

I this moment received Telegram from the other end of the Island (Gibbs Hill) stating Schooner "St. George" is on shore in Hog Fish Cut.—I have sent boats and hands to her, but will not be able to give you any information by this mail.

The "Cornubia" from Wilmington is coming in the ship channel, you will receive letters and papers in this mail, if there are any in her letter bag for you.

John T. Bourne.

St. George's, Bermuda
8th August, 1863.

I. H. Flanner Esq., Wilmington.

Dear Sir:—Enclosed you will please find Bill Ladg. for two cases shipped on board str. "Banshee," they are for John Treanor Esq., Savannah from James Mc.Hugh of Belfast, freight paid at Bermuda and for which McHugh will be valued on.—

Case No. 8 contains Felt Hats.
["   "] 9   do   Combs.   John T. Bourne.

St. George's, Bermuda
21st August, 1863.

Ed. Lawrence & Co., Liverpool.

Gentlemen:—I have the pleasure of sending you acct. of Disbursement sh. "Banshee" amt. to £734.9.5 and have to advise drafts on you to that amount.

The "Milicent" will leave early next week with the "Banshee's" cotton and please effect Insurance.—

I am happy to inform you that the "R. E. Lee" arrived here a day or two ago and reports that the "Banshee" arrived in safe after a passage of 4 days. The charges on reshipment of cotton will follow cargo.

John T. Bourne.

St. George's, Bermuda
22nd August, 1863.

Alexdr. Collie & Co., London.

Gentlemen:—Your favor per "Flora" is duly at hand and contents noted. As these Arms are in immediate requisition in the C. States I sent them in per "Flora" freight for which I presume will be settled by the agent on his arrival here next Tuesday. The "Flora" left yesterday.

I have shipped on board the Str. "Miriam" the cotton which I trust will arrive safe and in good order and meet a good market.—

I have to advise draft favor of 19th inst. favor of Walker £491.10.5 with others which in due time please protect. I will give you detailed statement of your business by "Harriet Pinckney" to sail in all next week, . . .

John T. Bourne.

St. George's, Bermuda
26th August, 1863.

Jn. B. Lafitte Esq., Nassau.

Dear Sir:—Your favor 27th, 28th and 30th are all at hand and I note contents.

The steamer "Elizabeth" arrived safely, landed her cotton and has again left for the Coast.—The "Dundee" has arrived and I put all the Coals on board the "Elizabeth" charging all expense of freight in her disbursements and you will charge her with the coals only.

Bacon.—There is a very large supply of Bacon and Pork in market, no freights have yet been taken; I do not think $900. will be taken payable inside.

I enclose Table showing the arrival and departure of mails, but there are always men of war going home and to Halifax, besides cotton str. with sealed mailed bags.

Str. "Eugenie" arrived into port yesterday with 400 bales cotton.—Str. "Spaulding" at Charleston, "Cornubia," "Venus," "Gibraltar," "Advance" at Wilmington, the "Gilbraltar" late (Sumpter) broke down and went through.

John T. Bourne

St. George's, Bermuda
26th August, 1863.

Ernest Zachrisson Esq., Nassau.

Dear Sir:—Your esteemed favor of 30th ultimo is duly at hand and note contents. There are several strs. running to Bermuda but I do not expect these will continue long as all the CS. property is now nearly run in.—

As the winter advances Woollen goods such as Blankets will be in demand, but as it is only known by the last str. going in to the States that goods can be bought here is the cause of no demand.—

Required, Cheap Bagging, Cheap Brandies in cases, say 30 @ 35/—per case short Enfield Rifles with cartridges to suit and Coals.—

John T. Bourne

St. George's, Bermuda
26th August, 1863.

Fraser Trenholm & Co., Liverpool.

Gentlemen:—Your esteemed favor of 2nd inst. is this day duly at hand and contents noted. Enclosed please find—

Second of N. S. Walker's draft for £7697.1.6 account reshipment cotton ex. schooner "St. George"; copy acct. disbursement str. "Elizabeth" in support of which Capt. Lockwood took with him.—

I have to advise drafts 20th August for Harrington Harvey, £150.—W. H. Grisit £100 [illegible word] £100 and C. Hai [illegible] £30—Edward Pietsch £80 which in due time please protect. "Gibraltar," "Lord Clyde," "Cornubia" all arrived at Wilmington; "Gibraltar" broke down before she get there and sailed through the blockdade, the enemy taking her for one of their own ships, this I heard from Eugenie arrived yesterday.

Ships "Ernestine" and "Elizabeth Jenkins" arrived but very insufficient for the market. Received a letter today from Mr. Lafitte. He says there is no coals at Nassau, the schooners I sent to Nassau on Fraser's acct. for Coals, has returned without any.—Mr. Lafitte has sent me up some Bacon but I fear I cannot do anything with it, our market is overloaded with all salt provisions.—

The steamers and sailing vessels have all made such a rush on me from Nassau that with small establishment I am almost unable to make headway. The CS. Property will all go in this month and musquets, short Enfields &c. are wanting the "Ella and Annie" will take the "Miriam's" cargo to Texas.—

Our island is very healthy and as the winter is coming I trust we will not be troubled with cruisers.—

Cotton is about 3,000 which will all be away to your port, say 25th September.

John T. Bourne.

St. George's, Bermuda
26th August, 1863.

Alexd. Collie & Co., London.

Gentlemen:—Your esteemed favor of 8th inst. is duly to hand with enclosures all of which shall have my attention in due time. By this mail you will receive acct. disbursement St. Venus amt. to £3060. which I trust on examination will be found correct.—I have to advise draft favor N. T. Butterfield for £1025, N. C. McCallan £150 and £300 which in due time please protect.—"Venus" has again arrived into Wilmington.

John T. Bourne.

St. George's, Bermuda
28th August, 1863.

Fraser Trenholm & Co., Liverpool.

Gentlemen:—Referring to my letters of 26th inst I have now to enclose charter party for cotton ex. "Elizabeth." Capt. Lockwood's cargo is now being shipped on board the "Florida" and I shall also send the balance of "General Beauregards"— Capt. Lockwood agreed to allow Capt. Simpson to take a full deck load.

I have to advise drafts, favor W. H. Grisit for £100—A. D. Barnard £369.15.10, Helen Maria Crispin £20 and Capt. Johns £[.........] all of which in due time please protect.

John T. Bourne.

P. S. You can credit me with 2½ pb. ton freight of cotton.
J. T. B.

St. George's, Bermuda
29th August, 1863.

B. & E. McHugh, Belfast.

Gentlemen:—I have now the pleasure to enclose account of reshipt. for two cases belonging to Mr. Treanor of Savannah showing expense incurred £79.19.10 which I have this day valued on you for in favor of Messrs. Shorter & Co. @ 10 days which please protect.—

No steamer running the blockade will take freight payable inside and as the articles were light, it was the most reasonable I could obtain, I am happy to say that they are all safely arrived in Wilmington.

John T. Bourne.

St. George's, Bermuda
18th September, 1863.

James W. Calder Esq., Liverpool.

Dear Sir:—In accordance with instructions from Messrs. W. C. Bee & Co. your friends in Charleston I have much pleasure in forwarding you the cargo of cotton landed ex. strs. "Ella and Annie" as per bills lading enclosed which I trust will reach you in safety.—The amt. of disbursements of the "Ella and Annie" amts. to £3106.17.10 to your debit against which I have valued on you as follows at 30d/s which in due time please protect.—Gosling Bros. £412., A. J. Musson £120., Louis John Crumpton £114.12., M. T. Fisher £84., Harrington Harvey £150., Helen M. Crispin £25., Wm. H. Grisit £100., A. J. Musson £200., £115., Grace Love £24. The expense incurred for reshipment will follow per str. "St. Thomas" who will leave this the early part of next week for your city.

John T. Bourne.

St. George's, Bermuda
18th September, 1863.

John Fraser & Co., Charleston.

Gentlemen:—Your esteemed favor of 31st instant come duly to hand per "Flora" and I note contents. I regret to learn the progress of the enemy but hope to hear of their utter defeat which is not improbable. We are in hopes that the length of time taken by the enemy to progress thus far, which amounts to nothing will deter them from making further attempts. Sebastopol held out against all anticipations and I trust Charleston will be able to do the same.—

Ere this reaches you, you will have heard of the safe arrival of the "Gladiator" in Liverpool.—

The Confederate Govt. have only about 1,000 bbls. of Gunpowder here which is a small quantity. I cannot say if they have any at Nassau. If you sell them your powder here you must add on 12 mos. storage @ 6c per bbl. per month or thereabouts.—

The "Florida" with coals arrived here from Nassau on 4th ultimo with 800 tons of coals which Mr. Walker purchased at £3. (Three pounds) per ton. The "Elizabeth Jenkins" arrived three or four days afterwards .and as I knew that the "Ernestine" was close up with other vessels from Nassau for Messrs. Collie str. and Mr. Campbell's from London with three other cargoes belonging to resident persons I could not obtain any more than the 50/— in 12 days after the arrival of the "Florida." I had bundled in on me all at once 35 sail of strs. and sailing from the coast Nassau and England, 7 of which were cargoes of coals not including the E. J. & Enste^{ne.}

The agents here for the Confte. Govt. not being business men do not wish to pay a liberal or even a market price and if it was not that I am afraid I may injure the cause in the Island, after making such strenuous efforts to carry out the wish of the Govt. I would give up having anything to do with them. I have received the draft for the Guns and Major Walker intended giving me the one for £15000 but he has been confined to his bed by illness the past week. No doubt I shall have it in time to forward early next week.

John T. Bourne

St. George's, Bermuda
24th September, 1863.

Alexd. Collie & Co., London.

Gentlemen:—Your esteemed favor of 5th inst is duly at hand and I note contents. I have handed over to Mr. Greig the Bills Lading as requested. Mr. G. is now convalescent having been suffering from cold and fever.

I have to enclose expense of reshipment of cotton ex. str. "Venus" forwarded per str. "Miriam" amt. to £507.8.6 to your debit and have to advise draft in favor Messrs. George R. Rankin and John C. Rankin each for £200 which in due time please protect.

I shall be always happy to afford Mr. Grieg any local information.

John T. Bourne.

St. George's, Bermuda
28th September, 1863.

Jn. & Thos. Johnson, Liverpool.

Gentlemen:—. . .[3] "Advance" arrived on Saturday from Wilmington; Charleston still holds out, and blockaders have been blown off in a storm.

John T. Bourne.

---

[3]Three paragraphs here omitted relate to the local market.

St. George's, Bermuda
12th October, 1863.
Per "Oleander" via New York.

Charles Wm. & Wentworth Gray, London.

Gentlemen:—Referring to my letter of the 3rd inst I have now the pleasure to enclose draft with bill lading attached for £5–90.7.7 on M. White Esq. which in due time he will protect, ere this reaches you this cotton will be well on its way to Liverpool and I trust Mr. White will receive profits of a high market; while on this subject I am happy to say all the cotton at Bermuda and Nassau is being now shipped and there are no prospects of any further arrivals at Bermuda or Nassau therefore the European markets must advance to higher rates than ever yet known. . . .

John T. Bourne.

St. George's, Bermuda
19th October, 1863.

Fraser Trenholm & Co., Liverpool.

Gentlemen:—Enclosed I have to hand you Bill Lading for 37 bales Cotton shipped on board the Bt. "Harkaway" for your port. This Cotton belongs to Mr. I. H. Flanner of Wilmington, N. C. who visited us in the "Advance" on her last voyage to Bermuda. He requested me to say, sell it to best advantage, and place the proceeds in the hands of Messrs. Baring Bros. & Co., London.

John T. Bourne

St. George's, Bermuda
21st October, 1863.

Fraser Trenholm & Co., Liverpool.

Gentlemen:—Enclosed I have now to hand you account sales and account with voucher showing proceeds of sale and expenses on the cotton saved from the late fire. You will also please find draft on Messrs. Char. Wm. & Wentworth Gray, London for £251.16.5 @ 30d/s for balance of acct. which I trust on examination will be found correct.

John T. Bourne

St. George's, Bermuda
24th October, 1863.

Fraser Trenholm & Co., Liverpool.

Gentlemen:—Enclosed please find B.L. per "Harkaway" for 10 bales Cotton xxx in red with letter from Thos. D. Walker Esq concerning same.—

Also in same B.L. Five (5) bales Cotton for acct. Col. Lamb for purchase of Guns which you, I presume, have instructions about.—Please insure.

John T. Bourne.

St. George's, Bermuda
26th October, 1863.

John White Esq., London.

Dear Sir:—I have the pleasure to inform you of the safe arrival this day of the str. "Advance" from Wilmington.

The cargo consists of Five Hundred Bales of Cotton which I would suggest to you to insure against fire while now in the course of reshipment and hope to forward you Bills Lading per good ship shortly.

The Marine Insurance will commence on signing Bill of Lading which will be duly notified.—

News—"Venus" lost on Wilmington coast. No further progress by the enemy on Charleston.

John T. Bourne.

St. George's, Bermuda
30th October, 1863.

Turner Bros. Hyde & Co., Northampton.   Via New York

Gentlemen:—Without any of your favors to reply to, I have now to inform you that I have effected sales of Calf Skins and small parcel of Shoes amt. to £700 at 25/—p.b. ton on invoice for which please find draft on Messrs. Charles Wm. & Wentworth Gray @ 60d/s of which they will be duly apprised.

You will ship me on your account for sale immediately any quantity of Calf Skins in packages of two or three doz. each, 10 doz. in a case is too unweildy; this shipment I would be glad to receive via Halifax, N. S. that I may meet my purchasers early in January also.

Cavalry long leg Boots in cases as before, the two packages have been disposed of; I am in heavy for the sale of the balance of Army Bluchers but you will be advised with remittance should I succeed in completing sales by mail.

John T. Bourne.

St. George's, Bermuda
19th November, 1863.

J. Stewart Oxley & Co., Liverpool.

Gentlemen:—Your esteemed favor of 31st ultimo is duly at hand and contents noted.—I regret I cannot advise further shipments of Cotton, the "Flora" arrived yesterday with Cotton from Wilmington and brings the news of Five captures out of seven blockade runners, therefore so far as Bermuda is concerned you may not expect to receive over 300 Bales in the next three months.

Please wind up all sales of Cotton in your hands vesting proceeds thereof in 50 Coils Manilla Rope and the balance in Bagging fit for Cotton Bales with invoice and account Cement, all to be insured and when you have [illegible] Blockade runners from England I will be able to ship more Cotton.

John T. Bourne.

Bourne Letter Book Number Three
November, 1863–May, 1864

19 Nov 1863

Messrs Collie, Westhead & Co.   Liverpool.

Gentlemen:—I have the pleasure to enclose Charter Party of Brig Lewellyn with a cargo of cotton for the order of John White Esq, Bill of Lading for which has been forwarded to him under cover to Messrs Alex Collie & Co; this cotton is to be sold & the proceeds placed to the credit of the State of North Carolina of which Mr White or Messrs A. C. & Co. will in due course direct you. (£25 deducted from freight to be credited to Mr Freig) I enclose letter to me from Capt Gibson for your guidance. The Brig will leave today. . . .

John T. Bourne

Nov. 23 1863

W. O. Massie Esq. New York.

Dear Sir:—Your favour of the 22nd ult is duly at hand & contents noted, I forwarded you the Certificate by the Harvest Queen wh. will enable you to obtain a release from the Bonds. As the Bonds are now imposed on the various importers from the States & the Oath which is necessary to take before the Consul makes it more profitable both for Soul and Body to confine our importations from England, although at a higher rate of freight & a longer period of obtaining them. Our Market at the present time is full of all kinds of Merchandise & I would not recommend any further shipments for the present. . . .

John T. Bourne

Nov. 27 1863

Fraser, Trenholm & Co. Liverpool.

Gentlemen:—I enclose draft for £75 which place to the credit of Mr. Seixas[1] of Wilmington, North Carolina. The

[1] J. M. Seixas, Confederate War Department agent at Wilmington, North Carolina.

steamers Coquette and Heroine leave during the coming week for the coast. I would call your attention to the publication in the New York Herald of the 16th instant (Nov) of the correspondence which has fallen into the hands of the Yankees. In the agreement of Messrs Reid & Co it appears as if they & the Agents of the Confederate Govt were for the future to receive the profits or rather that, that House & their friends are to have the option of purchasing supplies & selling cotton for the Govt.; thereby setting aside those who having passed through with them the doubtful Ordeal in the beginning of their struggle for Independence; the appointment of so many Agents by the Government to act for them seems to conflict their movements and their Agents being strangers in England make so many supposed friends that their business is actually known before they get to work. It was my intention to have opened a correspondence with Col Gorgas on this subject and suggest for the better preservation of secrecy the fewer appointments made in Europe and the Colonies the better. I am of opinion that the whole produce passing through Bermuda & Nassau into your hands can be disposed of by you and the proceeds vested in the various orders received from the Confederate States through Mr Mason or his duly accredited representative; by this means the Confederate Govt will not appear in partnership with an Mercantile jobbing house at present; their articles will come at a considerable cheaper rate & their steamers better suited for the purpose required. . . .

John T. Bourne

Nov. 28th, 1863

Thos. S. Begbie Esq. London.

Dear Sir:—I have your favour of the 30th ult; I trust ere this that the Harkaway with the Emma's cotton is with you & has realized a handsome profit; I regret to state that the Yankees have made wholesale captures—5 out of 7 of our Blockade runners have fallen into their hands. . . .

John T. Bourne

Dec. 2nd 1863

Messrs. W. C. Bee & Co & C. T. Mitchell & Co. Charleston.

Gent:—Herewith I have pleasure to enclose disbursements & Account current closing up the transactions of the steamer Ella & Annie at Bda. I have to acknowledge your letter of 2nd Nov. on wh. I have to remark that Mr Jervey & Capt Bonneau were right to represent matters to you as they appeared to them, but they should have pointed out to me personally their dissatisfaction in order that I may have remedied any neglect of mine, had any such really existed, but they both were fully aware that the first three days detention was caused by want of a Revenue Officer to attend agreeable to Law in unloading the vessel, for until such Officer could be provided by the Customs, it was totally impossible to remove one bale of cotton from the ship under penalty of confiscation, as in the case of the stmr. Herald, Capt Coxetter in October 1862; had Capt. Corbin called on me as he should have done, I could have proved to him that the principal detention, & finally the unfortunate disaster arose from the fact that while the ship was being laden and the Lighters were alongside in readiness to have their cargoes discharged on board, Capt Bonneau ordered them to cast off and follow him to the Port of Hamilton entailing additional expense & risk as before stated. This fact I apprehend was never communicated to Capt Corbin nor the further fact that the unnecessary carrying of the ship to Hamilton detained her at Bermuda one week namely from the 5th to 10th September on which day, as she proceeded to sea, she was plumply met by a Federal Cruiser just coming to the land; both being well within the specified limits & within reach of the common guns on the battery off St. Georges harbour, this of course turned her back into Port for shelter which caused further delay. Had Capt Bonneau taken in his cargo on one side & the water &c on the other, as the other ship did, I feel convinced that he would have been at sea all right on the 5th, four lighters being employed for that purpose. . . .[2]

---

[2]Two paragraphs omitted here discuss misrepresentations made by agents of the addressees.

I also regret that our business correspondence should thus terminate, but much more do I regret that you should have been subjected to such heavy loss by the capture of the Ella and Annie and I am convinced that had your interest in her been looked after as is the business of the highly respectable House of John Fraser & Co to whom I was indebted for an introduction to you, she would now have been in your possession.

John T. Bourne.

2nd December 1863

Jno Fraser & Co., Charleston.

Gentlemen: Your favour of the 28th Oct per Stmr Flora came duly to hand contents noted. On the receipt of your letter I personally offered to deliver over to Major Walker the Guns and Equipments & requested payment as you directed, but Major Walker declined to receive them, saying that he did not think they were in good order; in consequence of which I called a survey and wrote him on the subject (copy of correspondence herewith enclosed) and I have now to hand you original of same.

I regret to state that the Letter Bags of the Cornubia, Ella and Annie and R. E. Lee have fallen into the hands of the Yankees; how this happened I am unable to say; there were several letters in the E and A's bag for you & the others you received per Hansa. The N Y Herald published some of the correspondence & I enclose the sheet for your perusal; By Messrs Reid & Co's contract the Confederate Govt seems wishful of passing its business into other hands, by setting aside those mercantile men, who have passed through with them in the trying ordeal of the first stage of their Struggle for Independence; the publication of this contract with Reid & Co (which I fear is *too true*) tends to weaken the credit of the Government from the fact that it is a partnership and very badly managed; how much better it would be for the Govt to send all their orders for supplies into the hands of Messrs Fraser, Trenholm & Co through Mr Mason or his Deputy & dispense with their Agents; these Agents are no doubt good, patriotic and moral men, but not brought up to business habits and consider these apparent lucrative bargains beneficial. If the Confederate Govt is to own 2/3 of 5 Steamers surely it would be better to own the *whole* of *Four* & run them on their own account & risk; by this means they would avoid any collision with the jobbing Houses & be on a respectable & safer footing. The fewer Agents sent from the Confederacy to the Island and Europe the better; this would insure secrecy with men of business & the wants of the Confederacy supplied without the knowledge of the Enemy & their friends; from what we read in the papers, I fear all this trouble in England has arisen from parties sent from the Confederate States as lookers on, & aspiring to power, tell their errand to their new friends, before their work is complete. . . .

John T. Bourne

24th December 1863

S. Isaac Campbell & Co. London.

Gentlemen:—Your esteemed favours of the 28th Oct, Nov 26 & 27 are duly at hand, also Mr Hart's of 28th Oct & 26th Nov, the former guiding me relative to Mr Thorrold; Mr Hart's letter I handed to him; I must say the expense of living in Bermuda is higher now than I ever knew, properties which commanded little or no rent last winter, have gone up to fabulous prices and these prices are only paid by the strangers and non-Colonists. Your orders for the future will be attended to. Any gold coming to my care will be forwarded as you direct. The Harriett Pinckney has not as yet made her appearance & we are sorry to learn of her disaster; the City of Petersburg I learnt arrived safe in Wilmington and had left, but only took out to Nassau 5–600 bales cotton. The Ranger and Coquette both returned into port last week, having broken down just as they were going into Wilmington. We have no advices from the South.

John T. Bourne

15th February 1864

Thos A. Patteson Esq. Liverpool.

Dear Sir:—Your favour of 23rd ult is duly at hand & contents noted. The cargo of the Enterprise has been disposed of at Nassau. I have been unable to dispose of any of the goods; the fact is our trade with the Coast has considerably declined owing to the recent captures. I will wind the transaction up as soon as possible, as long winded accounts are always un-profitable. . . .

John T. Bourne.

19th Feb 1864

Girard & Gautherin.   Paris.

Gentlemen:—Referring to your instructions enclosing In-voice & B/L for 21 bales Grey Cloth I have to inform you that this Cloth has safely arrived and I have requested the agent for the Navy Dept to take it over, making me the payment as you requested, which he has declined to do, not having any instructions from his Dept to receive "Grey Cloth"; your contract which he holds specifies Grey Flannel and *ready made Clothing* for the Navy Dept; and the quantity of Flannel named is 50 M Yards; he has taken patterns of the Grey Cloth and sent them to Richmond and before taking it over will await instructions therefrom. The copy of the Contract shewn me by the C.S. agent requires the production of a certificate of the market value at Paris of the article received, signed by the C.S. Consul or agent. No such certificate has accom-panied your present shipment. . . .

John T. Bourne.

26th Feb 1864

Col James H. Burton, C.S. Army, Macon, Ga.

Dear Sir:—In accordance with your instructions conveyed in your letter of 22 Dec last I have delivered to Major N. S. Walker the 11 c/s steel for the C.S. Govt as per enclosed acct sales, net proceeds £268.11.2 wh[ich] I hold subject to your order. Please say what I am to do with the mirrors & other pkgs & let me know the sterling cost that I may pass them through the Customs. . . .

John T. Bourne.

27th Feb 1864

Marshall Beach & Co. Wilmington

Gentlemen:—Under date of 23 Jan Mr James Adger writes me relative to goods shipped by him on board Str Nola which were intended to be forwarded to you, but I regret to say that the Nola has been stranded and all these goods are a total loss. Mr. A. however, learning of this disaster & not knowing the final result requested that I should send forward to you the encl. invoice. The str Minnie is loaded & waiting for a pilot; the North Heath, Capt Burroughs is momently expected, also Capt Leslie. The str Jona bound to Bermuda en route for Wilmington has foundered in the English Channel. Trusting all will go right with the Confederacy in the Spring.

John T. Bourne.

2nd March 1864

Messrs B. Woolley Hart & Co. Nassau.

Gentlemen:—Without any of your favours to refer to, I have only to say that the goods sent here for Major Walker to purchase are still on hand, he having declined to take them; I have made repeated efforts to effect sale of these goods, but am unable to do so at any price. I have received orders to send in the shoes to Messrs Marshall Beach & Co but owing to the manner of paying freight in advance viz £30 to £40 per Ton I have been unable to comply. Trade is very dull & I see no prospect of disposing of these goods, the fact is the C.S. Govt have large supplies of woolen goods from England, all of which have arrived safe. . . .

John T. Bourne

5th March 1864

John Fraser & Co. Charleston, S.C.

Gentlemen:—This will be handed to you by Capt Hora of the Thistle who leaves this for Wilmington tomorrow, he will hand you the papers re. the ships cargo &c. I could not obtain a higher rate of freight from Mr Walker & private freight is small. I thought it better to take £30 a ton payable here than £40 payable inside.

As considerable feeling exists in Bermuda about taking in to the Confederacy, soldiers who have escaped from Federal Prison (and very useful men) in the steamers going in from time to time; will you be kind enough to give me authority to act in such particular cases with any ships in which you may be interested for this purpose. You are aware that these men have only what they stand in on arrival here from Halifax & as circumstances direct two or three of these men may be conveyed across to their corps with little expense to the owners of steamers which would only be their consumption.

Observing in your correspondence with the Govt relative to the Gunpowder I hope you will make provision for the storage here since August 1862 at 6d sterling per month for each barrel. Mr. Walker has not yet given me payment for the Guns but he has promised to do so; as far as I am able to judge, I do not think that Mr W has much means in England at present; say if you are to bear the storage of the Guns up to the time I deliver them to Major Walker. The reason I did not put any powder in the Thistle, I presume you have sold it, I therefore thought if anything happened it might injure the sale. The steamer Florrie returned into port yesterday in a sinking condition, she will be obliged to go to Halifax for repairs. Capt Maffitt of the Florida was in her. . . .

John T. Bourne

8th March 1864

Fraser, Trenholm & Co. Liverpool

Dear Sirs:—Capt Hora having succeeded after some delay in obtaining a Wilmington Pilot, the Thistle left here yesterday for Wilmington with about 100 Tons of freight. He put on shore to be sent to England by the first oppty his Chief Officer and one seaman.

John T. Bourne

18th March 1864

B. W. Hart Esq., London.

Dear Sir:—Your favour of the 19th ult duly at hand with enc. which I havve delivered to Mr Campbell who has again arrived from Wilmington with a full cargo of cotton; owing to necessary repairs the St Petersburg will go to Halifax this trip. Freights to the coast have considerably advanced therefore I have been unable to send in the shoes to Messrs Beach. Freights range from £30 to £40 payable in advance & little room at that rate. The odds are fearful against us through the blockade & I learn the change in the Confederate currency is very likely to bring down the price of all kinds of goods. . . .

John T. Bourne

19th March 1864

Fraser, Trenholm & Co., Liverpool.

Dear Sirs:—. . . *Steamer Thistle* By the arrival of the Index on the morning of the 17th inst. I learn from Mr Thompson (brother of the Pilot of the Thistle) that she was on shore close the guns of Fort Fisher; her cargo had been thrown overboard and she was perfectly tight and, as soon as the tide & weather would permit the coals would be removed & a steam tug sent to her assistance. The Index brings cotton to Mr. Campbell. . . .

John T. Bourne.

29th March 1864

Gurney Smeed Esq. Nassau.

Dear Sir:—In accordance with instructions recd by last mail from (England) Turner Bros & Co I have the pleasure to hand you invoice BL for the goods wh.[ich] I shipped on board the bearer. This invoice may have been sold but several of the trunks del'd the contents were not found to be like the sample. The leather & Army blucher boots you are likely to find immediate sale for among our friends. Please keep up a communication with me as I have instructions to send you what I cannot sell here. I have on hand Calf Skins and Cavalry boots. . . .

John T. Bourne.

4th April 1864

Jno Stewart Oxley & Co., Liverpool

Duplicate of my respects per Instrinsic. It would be better to sell these parcels immediately on arrival as cotton must fall considerably in price Charleston being now accessible for Blockade running. The prohibition of sundry paying articles which have hitherto been sent into the Confederacy will only effect those concerned in that line. . . .

John T. Bourne.

9th April 1864

To Lieut Joseph Fry, C.S. Navy.

Sir:—Having received from Mr Mallory, the Secy of the Navy of the Confederate States, a letter dated 28th January 1864, wherein he stated that orders had on that day been given for the shipment of cotton to meet the amount of my claim on the Govt for expenses incurred on Bullion remitted to Messrs Fraser, Trenholm & Co on their account. I immediately wrote those Gentlemen for a statement of those expenses and having subsequently rec'd from Mr. Mallory another letter dated 4th March wherein he says "you are referred to Lieut Joseph Fry, C.S. Navy who has been instructed to audit and state your account" I beg leave to enclose to you the statement as received by me from Messrs F. T. & Co by wh. you will see that the sum of £2954.6.8 is the sum for which I stand debited by them & consequently the C.S. are responsible to me for that amount with interest from March 17th with wh. interest you will see I am being chgd by F.T. & Co. . . .

John T. Bourne.

16th April 1864

B. W. Hart Esq. London.

(Extract) Steamer Minnie Capt. Gilpin has made a splendid trip bringing 700 & odd bales cotton & a good lot of Tobacco paying for Herself & the Emily. There was no news from the Coast.

[John T. Bourne]

16th April 1864

Turner Bros, Hyde & Co. Northampton.

Just learnt by H. M. Vesuvius arrived from Nassau that the str Greyhound had reached that port safely. The restrictions put on the Blockade trade by the Confederate Congress is likely to cramp all connected in this Trade. The present holders of Cotton Bonds are the only persons likely to do any business with the Confederacy.[3]

John T. Bourne

16th April 1864

Thos Stirling Begbie Esq.
Managing Dir of the Albion Trading Co. Ltd.

Dear Sir:—I last had this pleasure on the 7th inst. I am happy to inform you of the arrival here of the str Minnie from Wilmington with 700 bales & upward of cotton, consigned to Mr Thorrold, as I have just been told by Capt Gilpin. On the day after the arrival of the Minnie Mr Thorrold came to my office in company with Captains Leslie, Burroughs and Gilpin & enquired in a very offensive and dictatorial manner if I was prepared to continue to disburse the ships. I told him if he would endorse over the B/L of the Minnie's cotton to me for reshipment that I was prepared to do so. He abruptly answered: "I won't." I then said that I declined advancing any further. In your letter of the 26th December last in announcing to me the intention of sending out four steamers to run in the trade to Wilmington you say, "I have arranged at Nassau that the steamers if they go there are consigned to Hy Adderley & Co while Mr Atkinson manages the business, or at least is specially representing the Company and myself, I presume you will be happy to enter into a similar arrangement with me, Mr Thorrold occupying the position in Bermuda that Mr Atkinson does at Nassau, and not believing that you will otherwise than cheerfully accept the Agency on these terms, I send the steamers on to your care."—Again

---

[3]These restrictions were those imposed by the Confederate "blockade statutes." See introduction for discussion of trade regulations issued in March, 1864.

on the 25th January 1864 in your letter to me as Managing Director of the Albion Trading Co you in their name say "We trust that your best exertions will be used for our interest in the dispatch of our steamers and to the sending home (to our order) of all produce."

In consenting to accept the agency of the Company, to act in conjunction with Mr Thorrold, I of course, believed that the steamers were to be regularly consigned to me, as well as their cargoes for reshipment to your order, for no other construction can be put on your remarks as stated above. Since, therefore, Mr Thorrold has either received or assumed the whole authority in your business, were there no other objection, I should decline further to act in these matters, for under no circumstance whatever would I again, by acting in business with Mr Thorrold, subject myself to his arrogant and insolent manner, even if the vacillating and suspicious manner in which he acts, did not compel me to avoid any business transaction with him. . . .

John T. Bourne.

C. W. & W. Gray. London. 16th April (Extract) The restrictions put on the Blockade by the Confederate Govt are likely to shut out all speculators and the Govt taking the business in their own hands, holders of cotton bonds only will reap any advantage.

John T. Bourne

28th April 1864

Messrs S. Isaac Campbell & Co. London.

Dear Sirs:—Enclosed I beg leave to hand you B/L for 30 drums Tobacco shipped by Messrs E. Solomon & Co. Wilmington, N.C. on s.s. Minnie & consigned to me here for transshipment to you. The cotton by the Minnie being intended to be shipped on the Harriet Pinckney for Liverpool I secured room in her for your tobacco also & directed it to be put on board. To my great surprise previous to the removal of a single package I received a Bill for the freight thereof from Mr James Thorrold which I enclose herewith, who informed me that none of it would be delivered until the freight was paid. I of course refused to pay the freight before the delivery was complete. The result of the controversy has been that Capt Gilpin, Commander of the Minnie has shipped the tobacco pr Harriet Pinckney & taken a B/L therefor deliverable to T. S. Begbie Esq. Managing Director of the Albion Trading Co. Ltd. the owners of the Minnie one of which he has handed to me & which I now enclose to be by him transferred to you on the payment of the freight from Wilmington here. That you may be able to account for the procedure on the part of Mr Thorrold it is necessary for me to inform you that I was appointed by the Albion Trading Co agent for their four steamers, the Emily, Minnie, North Heath and Helen, to act as such in conjunction with Mr Thorrold. . . .[4]

John T. Bourne

10th May 1864

I. H. Flanner Esq. London.

Dear Sir:—Your kind letter of 15th ult is duly at hand covering order on Messrs. A. Collie & Co which is quite satisfactory. We have news today by the Thistle arrived from Wilmington every thing is in favour of the Confederates; a great Battle is going on and no doubt you will learn the result by the mail which take home this. With reference to the missing package I will I hope be able to settle it with Mr Zuill. . . .

John T. Bourne.

11th May 1864

Hon. S. R. Mallory, Secretary of Navy, Richmond.

Sir:—Major Walker having handed me for perusal your letter of the 23 April last to Lieut Joseph Fry, C.S.N. I beg leave to state in reply to your remarks to him respecting the amount of my draft on Messrs Fraser, Trenholm & Co. for £2774.0.5. that that draft was for amount of Bill of disbursements here of Str of War "Florida" and the expenses of transshipment of Bullion &c as will fully appear by reference to the

---

[4]The remainder of this letter gives further details of relations with Thorrold.

enclosed copies of accounts which I now have the honour of forwarding. . . .

John T. Bourne.

13 May 1864

Messrs Lane, Hankey & Co. London.

Dear Sirs:—Your esteemed favour of the 1st Feb enclosing inv. & B/L for cargo of coals shipped on board the Lady of the Lake on your acct, I received in due course & I have now to advise the arrival of that vessel here on the 2nd inst.

The season having so far advanced that the trade of the steamers to Wilmington being now expected to be principally to Bermuda instead of Nassau, in consequence of the prevalence there of fever during the summer months, which subjects them to quarantine at Wilmington after the 20th idem, I deemed it would be to the advantage of all parties concerned in the Lady of the Lake to order her in here & I hope shortly to be enabled to wait on you with acct sales of her cargo. Of her cargo I have as yet delivered of only 70 tons of coal at 50/ ton delivered to str Georgiana McCan & although there is at present a large supply in the market I anticipate an active demand very shortly. . . .

John T. Bourne

13th May 1864

C. W. & W. Gray   London.

[Dear Sirs:] As yet I have not been able to do anything with the gunny cloth, in consequence of the bulk of the cotton from the Confederacy being sent, during the winter months, through Nassau, as the summer advances however the transit will be through Bermuda, when the demand will increase here greatly. Besides a large fire at Wilmington having destroyed upwards of 6,000 bales of cotton there will be a large demand for bagging and I hope shortly to wait on you with account sales. . . .

John T. Bourne.

20th May 1864

E. W. Cole Esq. Atlanta. Ga.

I recently received a letter from our mutual friends Messrs John Fraser & Co of Charleston informing me that you had made enquiry of them respecting shipments of Cotton from the Confederacy to Liverpool, through Nassau and Bermuda, and I hasten to inform you, that it will give me much pleasure to attend to that or any other business you may require to be transacted at this Island. From the commencement of the War I have been the Commercial Agent of the Confederate Government, as well as the Agent of Messrs John Fraser & Co & Messrs Fraser, Thenholm & Co. of Liverpool, whose transactions have been very large & I have every reason to believe with great satisfaction to them. My charges to them for receiving & trans shipping cotton have been 8/ stg per bale & 5% commission on amount of money advanced for payment of freight from Wilmington, warehouse rent & other local expenses, & I will transact any business you have here, on the same terms which is much more favourable than the charges established here which is 2½% on the value estimating cotton @ 1/6 & 1/10 lb and tobacco @ 2/ lb. It is at the instance of Mr Welsman of the firm of John Fraser & Co who left here on the 16th Inst. for Halifax that I now address you. . . .

John T. Bourne.

Bourne Letter Book Number Four
February, 1865–April, 1865

Port St. Georges Bermuda
11th February 1865—

C. M. Allen Esq: United States Consul

Dr. Sir, Learning through Nassau that there is every probability of an Armistice being concluded on between the North and South—I have to request that you will be kind enough to ask the Secretary of State, whether during such Armistice being happily concluded, if vessels laden with Merchandize, such as Provisions, Dry Goods and Medicines, will be permitted to pass through the Blockade of any port in the Southern States—And such Documents being produced to you satisfactorily shewing that such Vessels have nothing Contraband of War on board such as Gunpowder, Arms &c:

John T. Bourne

Port St. George, Bermuda
24th February 1865—

Charles W. & W. Gray, London.

Dr. Sirs, Please pay to Capt. Pine Master Brig "Driving Mist" the difference of freight between the rates named on Bill of Lading for His Cargo on the number of pounds of Cotton delivered in Liverpool, and the (¾) Three farthings per pound as named in His Agreement.

You will deduct from the freight all (¾) Three farthings per pound, a Comms. of 5% thereon, being the usual charge at this port for obtan' the Said Freight—

John T. Bourne

St. Georges 2nd March 1865

W. C. Hyland Esq. St. Geo:

My dear Sir, In accordance with Mr. Deblois with I hand you Balance of Rent due to 28th Ultimo also Acct. Current—

In reply to His enquiry whether I would adhere to my offer of £1000 for the Wharf Stores I feel much obliged to our Friend for his refusal at that time—All Trade is now disposed of & things during the Year will settle down as heretofore— I fully explained to Mr. Deblois the defects of the Property which of course from year to year [increase?].

My lease expires 30th May next when if He should desire it I may take them for another year but not at the present rent—But Mr. D. is open for another offer; I will take the premises over on the 1st June next paying £700 (Seven Hundred pounds) in specie here, or be prepared to give it up to His purchaser, or Tenants if We cannot negotiate.

John T. Bourne

St. Georges 14th March 18— [1865]

Dear Mrs. Barr,

Your note of this morning is at hand. I was in hopes Mr. Barr would have been in Bermuda during the month—

I could not give Four Thousand pounds for the Stores & Rent them on those terms, as there is no prospect of their paying the interest of the Money—There will not be any trouble with the European Powers.—

As regards renting them after they are given up by Mess. Higgs & Hyland I could not, but supposing I am liberty to make an Offer; I would be willing to pay Mr. Barr £1,500 (fifteen Hundred pounds stg.) for them, which, is a fair price— No very heavy goods can be stored on the floors—

I intend giving up Mr. De B'lois Stores in June next, should He not agree with me for Rent—All the Steamers & Surplus goods are being sent to England as no more cotton can be brought out.

John T. Bourne

St. Georges 23rd Mar 1865

Gosling Bros: Hamilton.

Dr. Sirs, I have the pleasure herewith to enclose your Acct: Current shewing Balance in My favor £883:6/10 which I trust on examination will be found correct—

The business hitherto carried on in our Island is now considered to be at an end, and as I am closing up all those transactions connected therewith, I will feel obliged if you will make it convenient to settle this Balance either by payment here, or in London with Mess. C. W. & W. Gray which ever suits your convenience.

John T. Bourne

P.S. With reference to the preceding I am in hopes to close all up on 31st May next, which I hope will meet the accommodation of all—

J. T. B.

St. Georges 28th March 1865

Gosling Bros: Hamilton

Dear Sirs, Yours of yesterday 27th Inst is duly at hand and contents carefully noted, in reply to which I beg to say that I will be happy to receive (when it suits your convenience) any money on Account, but I cannot entertain any Arbitration in this business, as our bargain was clearly understood by each of us, which was as follows "that all Str: Bills for Goods which I could contract with you were to be placed at your credit, and further, that I was to influence all into your hands that I could;" The former I have done, and the latter I did from the very first, namely, the "Minho" Capt. Parke & Herald, Coxetter, down to the present and I trust not yet ceased—

When we made this bargain nothing was said by either of us about arbitrating or deduction, you took your chance; as I had hitherto been purchasg. of you for Steamers arriving to my address, your bargain was with a view to hold the business, which=with my assistance you have done, and no doubt will continue.

I cannot help remarking to you that a week or two after I told you the cargo, I had 20 Gls. Casks of Spirits, Brandy in Cases &c; which I had ordered for the express purpose of Supplying the Steamers, but having contracted with you, I did not consider it fair to supply them & have the Articles now in Store—

John T. Bourne

St. Geo: 26th April 1865

W. E. Zuill Esqr: Orange Grove.

Dear Sir, No doubt but that you have heard of the disastrous termination of Matters in the Confederacy; I presume all these Matters will be now smoothed over; Our trade having now returned to the Old line; and as you are desirous of winding up all your business, I would like to purchase Wellington Lot if you are disposed to Sell.

John T. Bourne

Letter Book of
Major Smith Stansbury, C.S.A.
June, 1863–November, 1863

Richmond Arsenal
May 14th, 1863.

Gentlemen: I enclose copy of a receipt of yours which I hold dated May 17th, 1862 for ninety-seven thousand four hundred and eighty pounds of scrap Iron, contract price fifty dollars per ton.

Has this transaction ever been settled by you? If it has, please give me the dates that I may trace it.

If it has not been deducted from your accounts, or paid by you, please send me a check for the amount.

Smith Stansbury, Lieut. Col.

Messrs. F. B. Deane Jr. and Son, Lynchburg, Va.
97,480 lbs. 43,518 Tons, which at fifty dollars per ton amounts to $2175.90
Copy of Receipt attached.

Lynchburg, May 17th, 1862.

Received of the Quarter Master's Department, Confederate States, through Assist. Qr. Mr. Captain Thomas R. Sharp, ninety-seven thousand four hundred and eighty pounds, (97,480) lbs. scrap Iron.

(Signed in Duplicate)   F. B. Deane Jr. and Son.

Endorsement—Contract price Fifty Dollars ($50.) per Ton, 2240 lbs.

Thomas R. Sharp Assist. Q.M.
Richmond, June 15th, 1862.

Richmond, June 4th, 1863.

Honble. James A. Seddon, Secty. of War.

Sir: I have the honor to acknowledge receipt of your letter of 1st June, notifying me that the President has appointed me to the temporary rank of Major, under Act No. 337.

I accept the appointment, and have reported to Colonel Gorgas as instructed.

In your letter of December 16th, 1862, I was notified that the President had promoted me to the rank of Lieut. Colonel. For my own credit I respectfully request a letter from you stating that my reduction of Rank has not resulted from Official misconduct.

Smith Stansbury, Major

St. George's, Bermuda
July 13th, 1863.

Mrs. Cecilia C. Todd, St. George's, Bermuda

Madam: Having inspected the premises adjacent to your dwelling in company with Major N. S. Walker and Mr. Campbell, I respectfully offer for the rent of the Warehouse rooms, the yards, sheds, the wharf, the Office fronting on Water Street now occupied, the rear office, the small room near this, now used as a chamber, and of which mention was made to you, (the three last rooms to be used only for Office purposes), the Sum of three hundred pounds (£300.) Sterling, for one year, with the privilege of renewal, and payable in quarterly instalments of Seventy-five pounds (£75.) each.

If notified before 9 o'clock on Wednesday the 15th inst., that my proposition is accepted, it will be considered binding; otherwise I shall be at liberty to make other arrangements.

It is also to be understood that if required, all stores now in the buildings be renewed, within one month after signing their agreement.

Smith Stansbury

St. George's, Bermuda
July 14th, 1863.

Major Caleb Huse.

Major: I have the honor to enclose herewith copy of letter of instructions from Colonel J. Gorgas, Chief of Ordnance, dated May 19th, 1863. Also copy of letter from Lieut. Colonel I. M. St. John, Chief of the Nitre and Mining Bureau, with Endorsement of Colonel Gorgas.

It is to the latter that I would respectfully call your special attention.

We are in urgent want of Saltpetre to keep our powder works at Augusta, Ga. in operation.

The capacity of the Mills is to produce five thousand pounds (5000) pounds per working diem of ten hours, or ten to twelve thousand pounds working day and night, and this could be nearly doubled by certain improvements.

The supplies of Saltpetre are from 1st Running the Blockade, 2nd The limestone caves of Va., Tenn., etc 3rd The Nitre Beds—

The last will hardly yield anything for a year to come, and the supply from No. 2 is very uncertain.

You are doubtless aware that it was the policy of the old U. S. Government to accumulate a Stock of this Material in time of peace, and a certain amount of money was annually appropriated for the purpose.

At the commencement of the war, the supply at the North was quite large, there being over two millions of pounds at Frankford Arsenal alone. The deficiency in the supply of lead has at times been very embarrassing, and the importance of having always on hand largely of this material, cannot be overestimated.

We are also in need of percussion caps, and it would be well to send over four or five millions as soon as possible.

I will show my letter to Major Walker before mailing it, and he will doubtless, add a line.

Smith Stansbury, Major

St. George's, Bermuda
July 20th, 1863.

Colonel J. Gorgas, Chief of Ordnance.

Colonel: The Steamer "Robt. E. Lee" has her Cargo, and is only waiting for Coal, of which we are now out.

Should she not leave within two days, she will probably be detained until about the 30th.

Owing to the crowded nature of the stores, and the difficulty of obtaining an additional Warehouse with an Office, it has been impossible to make out an accurate Inventory of Stores on hand.

Major Walker proposed an approximate Inventory to be prepared from the Invoices of Stores received here and trans-shipped, but as this would make me liable for all mistakes which may have been made previous to my arrival, I declined.

On a separate sheet I send a memorandum of some of the principal Stores remaining after the loading of the "R. E. Lee."

I have rented an Office and a Warehouse with a yard and Wharf adjoining, but we cannot get immediate possession. . . .

Smith Stansbury, Major

St. George's Bermuda, July 20th, 1863.
By Steamer "Robt. E. Lee," July 22nd, 1863.

Col. J. Gorgas, Chf. of Ord.

Colonel: Respectfully referring to a letter addressed to you by Lieut. Colonel I. M. St. John dated June 12th, and concerning the importance of shipping at least forty Tons of Lead, and sixty Tons of Saltpetre per month, and also of establishing a reserve of one thousand Tons of Lead, and Eight hundred Tons of Saltpetre.

A copy of the letter with your endorsement has been sent to Major Huse, and to our agent at Nassau.

In your endorsement you remark he (Major [Walker?]) will draw from Nassau all such Supplies as he can obtain there, and ship them over in the Government Steamers at the rate indicated as a minimum etc.

It is proper to inform you that there is rarely any direct communication between this place and Nassau.

Passengers leaving Nassau for Bermuda would generally pass through Charleston or Wilmington.

Smith Stansbury, Major

St. George's, Bermuda, July 20th, 1863.
By Steamer "Robt. E. Lee," July 22nd, 1863.

Lieut. Col. I. M. St. John, N. and M. Bureau

Colonel: Respectfully referring to your letter of 12th ultimo to the Chief of Ordnance in reference to shipping at least forty tons of Lead and sixty tons of Saltpetre per month, and of accumulating reserves of these materials.

Copies of your letter with the endorsements of Colonel Gorgas have been forwarded to Major Caleb Huse at London, and to our Agents at Nassau.

At present writing (after the loading of the "R. E. Lee") we have on hand, as follows—

—1500 Pigs of Lead, 100 lbs. each

—No Saltpetre—

You will be kept duly advised of the receipts and shipments to and from this Depot.

Smith Stansbury, Major

St. George's, Bermuda
July 23rd, 1863—

Major Caleb Huse, London.

Major: The Confederate Steamer "Florida" and the "R. E. Lee" (Giraffe) have been detained here several days for want to Coal, and for which we have been compelled to send to Halifax.

Our Steamers which run the blockade, at Wilmington, require the coincidence of a high tide to cross the bar—and of a dark night to evade the blockade.

The detention of a single day in their regular trips often involves the further detention of ten or twelve days, or greatly increased risk of capture —

I earnestly recommend, that seven hundred Tons of Cardiff coal be despatched here per month, to meet the prospective wants of our vessels, and that a reserve of two thousand Tons be accumulated as soon as possible to meet contingencies—

Smith Stansbury, Major

St. George's, Bermuda
Saturday, July 25th, 1863—

Col. J. Gorgas, Chf. of Ord.

Colonel: I enclose copy of bill of lading Steamer "Miriam," which arrived A.M. from Plymouth; This is the only document connected with the Ship's Cargo which has been received. The Steamer will commence discharging early on Monday morning, at the Wharf and Warehouse which I have just rented.

We have on hand here, (as previously advised,) about Sixty thousand Austrian Muskets, which, judging from the Samples I have seen, are also condemned Arms, and to us utterly worthless—

I am afraid that the Cargo of the "Miriam" consists of a number, or similar lot of trash—

I shall write to Major Huse by next Steamer, remonstrating against such purchases.

They have doubtless been made by Agents of his on the Continent, who are ignorant of our wants—

Smith Stansbury, Major

St. George's, Bermuda
July 29th, 1863—

Major: Mr. Greig, who has charge of the Steamer "Venus"— offers to carry eighty Tons of heavy freight to Wilmington for us, on the following terms—

Twenty five pounds Sterling per ton payable at Wilmington in a draft on London—The cargo to be at our risk, and the vessel at the risk of the owners—

If you think the terms fair, I will close with him, and the "Venus" can be loaded from the "Miriam" with Austrian Muskets, which are so much needed at home—

After some difficulty, I had one of the Cases opened yesterday, and was permitted to inspect one gun—

They are new and clumsy rifled Muskets, apparently of the manufacture of Liege, but, the case examined was in excellent order—

Smith Stansbury, Major—

St. George's—
August 1st, 1863—

Mrs. Cecilia C. Todd.

Madam: The Occupants of the front Office (Mess. Pickering &c. Co.) stated to me that their lease did not expire until 3rd October, and claimed that they would then be entitled to a notification of 6 months before being obliged to leave—

If this is the case I beg leave respectfully to suggest that a notification be immediately given—

S. Stansbury—

St. George's, Bermuda
August 3rd, 1863—

John T. Bourne—

My Dear Sir Please freight the "Banshee" as follows— 490 Pigs Lead, 25 Tons, 400 Cases Austrian Rifles, 50 [tons], 400 Boxes Ammunition, 25 [tons.] 100 [tons].

There will be sixty tons of lighter materials which I will select and advise you—

Smith Stansbury, Major

St. George's, Bermuda
August 3rd, [1863]

Col. J. Gorgas, Chf. of Ord.

Colonel: I enclose copy of bill of Lading, Steamer "Miriam," which arrived here July 25th from Hamburg, via Plymouth.

A portion of her Cargo is now being transferred to the Steamer "Venus" which will probably leave, as soon as she can be coaled, for Wilmington.

The balance of the Cargo will be stored.

We have received no cargo book or Invoice of Stores by the "Miriam."

In another letter I will send Invoice of Stores forwarded by the "Venus."—

Smith Stansbury, Major

St. George's, Bermuda
August 4th, 1863—

Major N. S. Walker

Major: Your favour of this date has been received containing suggestion in relation to the balance of freight for S.S. "Banshee"—

I feel sure the Major who is unwell, will heartily approve of this method, more especially, as the goods mentioned, are all greatly needed, *especially Alcohol* and *linseed Oil*, not to speak of the advantages of not removing the "Banshee" or disturbing the cargo of the "Gibraltar"—

George G. Gibson

St. George's, Bermuda
August 5th, 1863—

Mr. John T. Bourne

Sir: Please let the "Banshee's" freight be as follows—

300 cases Austrian Rifles, 400 Boxes (A.) Ammunition nearly all loaded, 498 Pigs Lead, 40 Tons *about* of cargo "Gibralter," all she has, and let the Ammunition from Penno's Store be transported to her boats.

Please freight the "Eugenie" and "Lady Davis" (Cornubia) at Penno's Wharf, as follows—the balance of Cargo to be made up of light goods to be hereafter designated—[:] 150 Austrian Rifles, 141 Cases Enfield, 300 Boxes Ammunition, "Eugenie," 250 Pigs Lead, 400 Cases Austrian Rifles, 500 Boxes Ammunition, "Lady Davis," 300 Pigs Lead.

Smith Stansbury, Major

St. George's, Bermuda
August 5th, 1863—

Surg. S. P. Moore, Surgn. General, Richmond, Va.

Sir: I arrived here on 8th July, and have since purchased under your Order of May 29th,

300 Cases of Brandy of Mr. J. T. Bourne @ 35/—a case—£525—

547 Gallons Brandy of Mr. J. W. Musson @ 16/— per gallon—£437.12.—

These will be forwarded to Wilmington as soon as the transportation can be spared.

At present my Orders from the Chief of Ordnance for Arms, Ammunition, and Laboratory Stores, are so imperative that I cannot send over the brandy.

Smith Stansbury, Major

St. George's, Bermuda
August 7th, 1863—

Col. J. Gorgas, Chf. of Ord—

Col.: Please receive under separate cover, "Invoices" with copies of Bills of Lading attached, from Mess. S. Isaac Campbell & Co. of London, of the Cargo of the Ship "Coral Isle"—

The Ship has not yet arrived in Port, but may be expected daily—

The Invoices &c—have been copied here, and are sent you by the special direction of the Mess. C. & Co.—

The "Harkaway" containing a Cargo of
    50 Cases Shoes
    30   "   "   Ordered to Major Waller
     9 Bales Flannels   Q. M. R—Va—
is in the harbor—

The "Gibralter" from London (S.I.C. & Co.) [S. Isaac, Campbell] has supplied the "Banshee" with a portion of her Cargo, (as per Manifest,) the balance consists of 980 Tons of Lead, 45 Casks of Pickaxes, for Engineer Bureau, and sundry chemicals for Major Waller [Mallet] Supt. of Laboratories.

Please find enclosed List of Cargo of "Banshee"—

Smith Stansbury, Major
Geo. G. Gibson

St. George's, Bermuda
Augst. 10th, 1863—

Major Caleb Huse, London.

Major: Please purchase and ship as soon as possible 10,000 lbs. of strong hemp twine, [.] 6 to [.] 8 In. inches diameter for fixing field ammunition.

Smith Stansbury, Major.

Concerning the Same—

Major N. S. Walker

Major Please forward the above unless you have reasons for withholding it—

I would recommend that you order the further purchase, in Halifax of five or ten thousand pounds of Strong hemp Twine, 06 to 08, In—[inches] diameter.—

Considering the risks of transit we ought to have a Stock on hand—

Smith Stansbury—

St. George's, Bermuda
August 10th, 1863—

Col. J. Gorgas, Chief of Ord., R[ichmond]. Va.

Colonel—Respectfully referring to your 22nd Ulto: about hemp twine.

We have none on hand. Major Walker had already ordered 5000 lbs. from Halifax.

I have ordered the purchase 10,000 lbs. more by Major Huse and requested Major Walker to purchase more in Halifax.

Considering the risks of transit we ought to have a Stock on hand—

Smith Stansbury, Major

St. George's, Bermuda—
August 11th, 1863—

Meajor Caleb Huse

Major: Referring to my letter of 14th Ulto: requesting the purchase of four or five millions of percussion caps immediately—I beg to request the purchase in addition of five millions.

The demand is great, and the supply here exhausted.—

We need immediately Carbines (for Cavalry), Revolvers (for Cavalry), Equipments (for Cavalry), Saddles &c.—&c.—

Smith Stansbury, Major

St. George's, Bermula
August 11th, 1863—

Col. J. Gorgas—

Colonel: Referring to your letter of 22nd Ulto: about sending arms &c. to Texas, We can supply all except the following—
2000 Cavalry Arms ....None on hand—
500 Revolvers ....   "   "   "
Mess. Klingender &c Co. wrote to Major Walker that they
had received 30 Boxes Revolvers too late to ship by the "Sumpter" (Gibralter) but would forward by next "Steamer"—Percussion Caps we have none. In my first letter to Major Huse,
I begged him to send 4 to 5 millions as soon as possible today—
I have thought it best to duplicate the order.—
English Saddles ....None
Equipments ....Only numnahs and Blankets.
Armorer and Blacksmith tools we will receive a Supply by
the "Coral Isle," daily expected.
You direct that the Boxes be opened, and the arms oiled
before shipment. This I fear will be impossible—
In a future letter I will endeavour to give you an idea of
the lack of facilities for work of all kinds here.—

Smith Stansbury, Major

St. George's, Bermuda
August 11th, 1863.

Col. J. Gorgas.

Colonel: Referring to your letter of 26th Ulto: about the
600 pdr. guns.
In my letter of 7th August, I advised you of the Cargo of
the "Gibralter" a portion of which was transferred to the
"Banshee."—
The "Gibralter" is still here with her guns on board, but
when she will leave I cannot tell. She is coaling now.
The Captains of the different vessels have great difficulty
with their Crews, as to wages and privileges, and I think that
these matters have been unwisely tampered with by Mr.
Seixas, at Wilmington.—

For your further information I would respectfully refer you to the Captains of the Steamers, running between here and Wilmington.

Some officers here should be clothed with plenary powers in all matters, where the Confederate States have authority, and I suggest Major Walker as immediately qualified.—

Smith Stansbury, Major.

St. George's, Bermuda
August 11th, 1863—

John T. Bourne,
    Please Load the "Advance" with
        500 Pigs Lead .... 25 Tons ....
        Light Freight .... 25 "   ....
for the latter you may send whatever comes nearest to hand—
say Cartridge paper, numnahs, bales of Blankets, &c.

Smith Stansbury, Major

St. George's, Bermuda
August 12th, 1863—

Col. J. Gorgas.
    Colonel: If not already done, please send me if possible, the three clerks asked for in my letter of 30th Ultimo.

The business cannot be conducted here with anything like system without a Corps of at least half a dozen first class clerks between Major Walker and myself.—

At present Major Walker has $1\frac{1}{4}$ and I have one—

The mere duplication of writing in my own Office could hardly be performed by a race-horse clerk working twelve hours a day.—

The three men asked for are worth more than any dozen that could be engaged here, and with the additional advantage that they are of tried fidelity.—

Smith Stansbury, Major

St. George's, Bermuda
August 12th, 1863

Mr. J. T. Bourne.

My Dear Sir: Understanding that the "Advance" belonging to the State of N. Car. is about to leave this Port for Wilmington, N. Car. and that her Cargo is incomplete and further that she is under obligations to carry over for the Confederate States a certain Amount of freight, I beg to know what portion of the enclosed list she can carry.

Smith Stansbury, Major

St. George's, Bermuda
August 13th, 1863—

Col. J. Gorgas, Chf. of Ordnance.

Dear Friend: Please purchase and send me One Copy Ordnance Manual—One Copy Army Regulations.

The latter is for my own use, the former I wish to present to Mr. Penno, the Proprietor of our principal warehouse.

He is warmly southern in his feelings, has treated me with great kindness, and attention, and has expressed a desire to have a Copy of the book—

If they can be sent free of charge so much the better.—

Smith Stansbury, Major

St. George's, Bermuda
August 13th, 1863—

Honble. C. G. Memminger, Secty. of Treasury.
    Through Chf. of Ord.

Sir: I have the honor to forward by Steamer "Eugenie" Captain Fry—one Box, Marked T.D. containing a Seal received from Mess. Frazer Trenholm and Co. Liverpool England.

The box is addressed to you, care of J. M. Seixas, agt. of War Department, Wilmington, N. Car—

Smith Stansbury, Major.

(Private)

St. George's, Bermuda

Augt. 13th, 1863—

Major M. Morfit, Wilmington N.C.

Major: I have received your letter of 30th Ultimo. enclosing one for Miss Fanny B. Morfit, Baltimore, M.D. I will forward it to Halifax, and hope it will reach its destination.

Smith Stansbury, Major.

St. George's, Bermuda

August 14th, 1863—

Col. J. Gorgas.

Colonel: Three Steamers left here yesterday for Wilmington.—The "Lady Davis," "Eugenie" Lord Clyde, ("Advance"). By the two former I sent letters.

The "Ella and Annie" arrived yesterday morning. I have received your letter of 6th in relation to her Texas Cargo. Referring you to my respect of the 11th on the same subject, we have on hand 584 Cases of the Arms, Austrian Muskets, which arrived by the "Miriam" and, which are in excellent order.—

It will require about three days to discharge her Cargo, and as many more to load and coal her.—

In the meantime I am in hopes that the deficient stores will arrive from abroad.—

Smith Stansbury, Major.

St. George's, Bermuda

August 16th, 1863—

Capt. S. G. Porter.

Captain: I regret the necessity of removing the Ammunition from the "Phantom" and more particularly the annoyance which it occasions to yourself.—

My instructions to Mr. Hawthorne who has charge of loading the Steamers were very explicit.—

Four hundred boxes of Ammunition must be reserved for the "Ella and Annie," send the remainder by Steamers now waiting for freight to Wilmington.—

You will very much oblige me by furnishing the following information.—

Exclusive of the necessary amount of coal, what is the capacity of your Steamer for carrying freight in tons of 2000 lbs.—

Supposing the freight to be in bulk, how many cubic feet, or cubic yards, can be conveniently stowed in your vessel.—

Supposing the Steamer to be loaded, how much of her cargo would you desire to be dead weight.—

Smith Stansbury, Major.

St. George's Bermuda
August 17th, 1863—

Mr. J. T. Bourne.

Sir: Please load the Steamer "Ella and Annie" at Mrs. Todd's Wharf with.—500 Cases Austrian Rifles, 480 Boxes Austrian Ammunition, 20 Carboy's Nitric Acid, 10 Carboy's Sulphuric Acid, 10 Carboy's Muriatic Acid, 1 Case Gum Shellac, 5 Casks Surgical Instruments, 50 Cases Saddlery, Emery, 10 kegs Horse Shoes.

Smith Stansbury, Major.

St. George's Bermuda
August 17th, 1863—

Mr. John T. Bourne.

Sir: Please load the "Elizabeth" with the following Cargo: 250 Cases Austrian Rifles, Cases Austrian Ammunition Ad-libitum. The balance of her freight will be hereafter designated.

Smith Stansbury, Major.

St. George's, Bermuda
August 18th, 1863—

Major Caleb Huse, London.

Major: I enclose copy of a letter from Col. Gorgas.

Since the fall of Vicksburg, the Trans-Mississippi Department will have to be supplied by direct shipments to Texas, and I presume out of Stores drawn from this point and Nassau.

Of the supplies ordered by Colonel Gorgas, I have on hand none of the following—Cavalry Arms (say Carbines), Revolvers, Officers' Swords, Cavalry Swords, English Saddles, Percussion Caps.

As soon as I can make out a correct inventory of the Stores here, I will forward a copy for your guidance.—

Smith Stansbury, Major.

P. S. I think it will be unnecessary to send you copy of the inventory. Another Steamer leaving for Wilmington will probably clear us out of all stores here, and we shall only have the cargo of the "Coral Isle" which is daily expected.

S. S.

St. George's Bermuda
August 18th, 1863—

Col. J. Gorgas.

Colonel: The despatch of another Steamer to Wilmington will so reduce our Stores that I hope it will enable me to make out the Inventory, which I so much desire to send you.—

The "Coral Isle" with an assorted Cargo, is daily expected.—

I have written to Major Huse, explaining our most urgent wants, and that the Trans-Mississippi Department will have to be supplied from this point, and from Nassau, by direct Shipment to Texas.—

You have doubtless given Major Huse instructions.—

The copy of "Coral Isles" invoice has been forwarded to you.—

Smith Stansbury, Major.

St. George's Bermuda
August 18th, 1863—

Col. J. Gorgas.

Colonel: Unless we receive a supply of percussion Caps before the "Ella and Annie" is ready to leave for Texas, I shall with the concurrence of Major Walker detain her for two or three days.

It is distracting to think that the Arms and Ammunition sent by her may be almost useless, without a supply of Caps.—

Smith Stansbury, Major.

P. S. I am very glad to inform you that the Austrian Rifles, which were on hand when I arrived, have turned out much better, than the samples I inspected led me to suppose.—

With careful cleaning by the soldiers, most of them will, I hope, turn out effective weapons.—

St. George's Bermuda
August 20th, 1863—

J. M. Seixas Esq., Agt. of War Dept., Wilmington N. C.

Sir: Packages of the following marks and numbers are to be forwarded as indicated below.—

50 Cases Shoes	From Major J. B. Ferguson Manchester England to
9 Bales Flannel	Major R. P. Waller Qr. Master Rd. Va—

J. C. & S. Packages of the following marks to be forwarded as indicated below.—

E. B. From John M. Robinson London England to Colonel J. F. Gilmer Engineer Bureau, Richmond Va.—

$\frac{S.S.}{E.B.}$ From John M. Robinson London England to Mr. D. H. Bur Supt. of Southside Rail Road Co. Petersburg Va.

Some of these goods will doubtless be shipped by the next Steamer arriving at your Port.

Please advise the parties as requested within.

Smith Stansbury, Major.

P. S. Important. The goods marked E. B. for S.S.R.R.Co. are to be charged with what you consider fair rates of freight. The fact that they were included with the E. B.'s in the list of Cargo of the "Gibralter," in which they were shipped, and the tonnage of the whole only given together with the misfortune of our entire want of weighing facilities prevents me from furnishing weights or measurement. Although it seems unfair to throw the burthen upon you, I must expect you to have them ascertained, and make the proper charges &c.

List of Goods offered for sale by Mr. Bourne.

August 25th, 1863—

20 Cases each containing 20 long Enfield Rifles with Bayonets, Scabbards, Snap caps, ramrods and stoppers complete @ 80/—per Rifle—

25 cases each containing 2000 Cartridges to suit above @ 70/—per M.

300 or 400 Boxes Superior Brandy for Family use @ 41/—per case. Cases Army Boots, Assorted Leather.

All which may be shipped on "Lee" and "Eugenie."

John T. Bourne

Major N. S. Walker.

Major: I recommend the purchase of the arms and ammunition at the prices stated, and of the army boots and leather according to your judgment.

For the Brandy I will make a bid, having a large order from the Surgeon General.

Smith Stansbury, Major.

Macon Georgia
August 25th, 1863—

Major Mallet

Needs: Serge, nitric acid, nitric strontia, lead, twine and thread.

Respectfully referred to Major N. S. Walker, for notice and return of paper—

3 Cases of Nitric of Strontia sent by "Banshee."

Smith Stansbury, Major.

St. George's, Bermuda
July [August] 26th, 1863—

Major N. S. Walker.

Major: In reply to your letter of 25th, Please rent by all means "Hunter's" premises; as to the price, your judgment is infinitely superior to mine.

For whatever you agree, as to the rent, I will certify to the quarterly accounts.

Smith Stansbury, Major.

St. George's, Bermuda
August 26th, 1863—

Col. J. Gorgas.

Colonel: The Steamer "R. E. Lee" arrived on the 19th, with letters from you of 1st, 3rd, 4th, and 5th August.

In reply to yours of the 1st—In my first interview with Major Walker, he informed me that there were on hand about 50,000—Austrian Rifles, "In horrible condition, and hardly worth storage room."

In the memorandum which accompanied my letter of 20th, July, I quoted his exact words.

Major Walker remarked that these arms were part of 100,000 purchased by Major Huse of the Austrian Government, and that they certainly never would have been sold but for the inferiority.

My inference was, that they were condemned Austrian Arms.—

They turn out to be fair guns, as explained in my letter of August 18th; In a future private letter I will give you an account of the embarrassments and difficulties which surround Major Walker and myself here.

Smith Stansbury, Major.

St. George's, Bermuda
August 27th, 1863.

Mr. John T. Bourne.

Sir: Please commence loading the "R. E. Lee" tomorrow, 200 Cases Austrian Rifles (if that number remain without affecting the 500 Cases for "Ella and Annie") you will find, say 580 in Mrs. Todd's Warehouse in all. 500 pigs of lead, if the Captain can carry it, 300 Barrels of Gunpowder, *without fail*. Such other light freight as may be hereafter designated.

Load the "Eugenie" with as much lead as she can carry, and 300 Barrels of Gunpowder. Very important.

Smith Stansbury, Major.

St. George's, Bermuda
August 28th, 1863—

Mr. John T. Bourne

Sir: Please ship by "Robert E. Lee" Two (2) *Hogsheads Sugar*. There are some tierces in Penno's Store. Please be particular about this, they are especially needed.

Smith Stansbury
Geo. G. Gibson

St. George's, Bermuda
August 28th, 1863—

Mr. J. M. Seixas, Agt. War Dept.

Sir: Your List of Distribution of Cargoes have been handed me by Major Walker.

The following are missing.

"Cornubia" left Bermuda December 2nd, 1862.
    Do.   "   "   February 28th, 1863.
    Do.   "   "   March 27th, 1863.
"Genl. Beauregard" "   (No date given.)
"Emma"   July 6th, 1863.

It will assist in the endeavour to straighten the papers at present in total confusion if you will furnish Duplicate of them.

Smith Stansbury, Major.

P. S. (Personal.) I had the pleasure of meeting your little Nephew. He leaves tomorrow in the "H. Pinckney," under the charge of Mrs. Greenough.

G. G. Gibson.

St. George's Ba.
August 28th, 1863—

Mr. J. M. Seixas, Agt. of War Dept.

Sir: In obedience to your request by direction of Colonel Gorgas I ship you by Steamer "Eugenie" 2 Hogsheads (two) of Sugar for the Ordnance Bureau.

Smith Stansbury, Major.

St. George's Ba.
August 31st, 1863—

Capt. [John] Wilkinson
Captain: Please receive 8 Cases Marked as follows—
4 Cases Engineering Instruments, 4 Cases Stationary.—

Smith Stansbury
Geo. G. Gibson.

St. George's Bermuda
September 1st, 1863—

Colonel J. Gorgas
Col: Your telegram of 21st Ulto. to Fort Fisher was received; in hand, just in time for the "Eugenie."

A copy was enclosed to Capt. Fry, and handed to me—

I send by "R. E. Lee" 300 Barrels Gunpowder, By "Eugenie" 300 Barrels Gunpowder.

We have left about 1400 Barrels which will be shipped by the first opportunity.

Smith Stansbury, Major
Per Geo. G. Gibson

St. George's Ba.
September 1st, 1863—

Col. J. Gorgas—
Col. The "Ella and Annie" has been detained coaling up to this time: She commences loading today with: 500 Cases Austrian Arms=12,000 arms, 484 Cases Austrian Ammuntn.= 484,000 rounds, 4 Cases Percussion Caps=400,000 (all we have). The caps were accidentally and providentially discovered, having been represented as other Stores. 12 Carboys Nitric Acid, 1 Case Gum Shellac, Medicines, Surgical Instruments, Cavalry Equipment &c, &c, &c (full List of Cargo will be furnished hereafter—).

Every precaution has been taken to load her with the greatest despatch, the greater part of her Cargo, being in a Schooner, out in the harbor ready to go alongside.

Smith Stansbury, Major
Per G. G. Gibson

Copied at St. George's Ba.
C. S. of America
War Dept.
Richmond Sept. 7th, 186—[3.]

Major Caleb Huse, 71 Jermyn Street, London

Major: Purchase and ship first opportunity to Bermuda Five thousand (5,000) pounds of Fish, or white Bonnet Glue for making fuse Cases.—We are in urgent need of it; as we have found that no substitutes, yet tried, will answer.

J. Gorgas,
Col. and Chf. of Ord.

Major Stansbury will purchase and ship, if it can be found in Bermuda, two thousand (2000) lbs. of glue, as advised, "Bonnet glue."—

St. George's Bermuda
September 5th, 1863—

Col. J. Gorgas.

Colonel: We have on hand—Lead, about 150 Tons; Powder, about 1,000 Barrels; Cases of Leather, about 150 Cases; Ingot and Sheet tin, quite a quantity.

I have again written to Major Huse to send Arms, Ammunition, Cannon Powder, Saltpetre, Lead, and Percussion Caps—

Smith Stansbury, Major.

St. George's Ba.
Sept. 5th, 1863—

Major C. Huse, London.

Major: Please forward as rapidly as possible: Arms, only 150 Cases on hand; Ammunition, none on hand; Lead, only 150 Tons on hand; Saltpetre, none on hand; Percussion Caps, none on hand; Cavalry Arms and equipments, say Carbines, Revolvers, Cavalry Sabres, etc., None on hand.

Of cannon Powder we have on hand about 1000 Barrels, but I have orders from Colonel Gorgas to ship Cannon Powder as fast as possible.

The departure of two or three Steamers to Wilmington with Powder, as part of their cargoes will clear us out. A supply should be forwarded at once. I think a considerable portion of it should be "Mammoth Powder"—for heavy guns—The powder for Field Guns might be marked F. that for heavy guns H.

Smith Stansbury, Major.

St. George's Bermuda
September 10th, 1863—

Mr. Campbell.

Dear Sir: Your kind offer to receive Two Tons of Lead on board the Stmr. "Juno" has been communicated to me.

I have given directions for Twenty Pigs to be delivered.

Smith Stansbury, Major.

P.S. Please direct the Captain of the Vessel, to deliver the same to Mr. J. M. Seixas, Agt. War Department, Wilmington, N.C.

It may be in my power to reciprocate this kind favor hereafter.

St. George's Ba.
September 10th, 1863—

Mr. J. W. Musson.

Dear Sir: Your favor of 8th Instant with samples of Brandy and Whiskey has been received.

I do not think the quality justifies the purchase for Medical purposes.—

S. Stansbury, Major.

St. George's Ba.
Septr. 10th, 1863.

Col. J. Gorgas.

Colonel: Referring to the promise in my letter of 20th [26th] Ulto:—

We have four Warehouses Penno's, Musson's, Doctor Hunter's, and, Mrs. Todd's, attached to each Warehouse is a Wharf.

The other Warehouses and Wharfs of the town are in private hands.

Only one Steamer can occupy a Wharf at a time.—Only four vessels, whether public or private, can be discharged or loaded at the same time for the reason that a Custom House officer is required for each vessel, and there are only four "Custom H." Officers. Several detentions have occurred from this cause since I have been upon the Island.

For a reason which I will explain in a future private letter, the Wharfs here are different from any that you have probably ever seen—

Commencing at the foot of the talus, and at about low water mark, the Bottom Shelves gradually out, into deep water. A vessel drawing ten or twelve feet cannot approach a Wharf, within less than 30 or 40 feet.

To load or discharge a vessel, gangways have to be rigged and unrigged, and this, with their poor appliances, is generally the work of a day—but the loss of a day, most frequently involves the loss of a moon—So that if even a second Wharf were vacant, as a general rule, a vessel cannot be loaded partly from one Storehouse, and partly from another. Neither can the Stores be transported from one Store-house to another; as there are no carts or drays: I do not think we could depend upon hiring half a dozen for a single day in St. George's—

The last difficulty is in part obviated, by a recent purchase of a small Schooner, by Major Walker—but the process of transferring by this means, is very slow.

We cannot open boxes of Arms, and clean and oil them etc. or do any work of the kind—No room—no workmen—no tools—no conveniences—This is not a City nor a town, but a village.—

Smith Stansbury, Major.

St. George's Ba.
September 12th, 1863

Col. J. Gorgas.

Colonel: Referring to your letter of 29th, Ulto:

The two promised Clerks Mr. George P. Black, and Mr. Gustave Alexandre, will find plenty of work to do.—

The salaries to which you propose to limit them $700. to $800. is utterly inadequate to their support.

The cost of living here, I estimate at fully 25% above that of N. York.

Without going into a statement of the cost of Provisions and clothing: The cost of very indifferent board, with the most slender accommodations, is about *one dollar* and *fifty cts.* per day, but [by?] the year—and difficult to procure at that.

Smith Stansbury, Major.

St. George's Ba.
September 14th, 1863—

Colonel J. Gorgas.

Col.: Referring to your letter of 28th, Ulto: about saltpetre and powder, I am sending over by every Steamer 300 Barrels of powder about as much as ought to be risked at a single trip.

I have acquainted you in previous letters of my demands upon Major Huse for Lead, Arms, Ammunition, percussion Caps—Powder etc.

I wrote Major Huse from Wilmington with a copy of your instructions, and a statement of our most pressing wants. Up to the present writing I have not received a line from him, doubtless the result of bad Mail arrangements, and no fault of his—

Smith Stansbury, Major.

St. George's Ba.
September 14th, 1863—

Colonel J. Gorgas.

The "Ella and Annie" for Texas started September 9th from Hamilton, was chased into St. George's by a Yankee Man of War;—started again on September 11th, '63, encountered a terrific gale and this morning came in with paddle boxes carried away, and otherwise damaged—

The Captain expresses the fear that two months may elapse before the necessary repairs can be made—

The Cargo of Arms, I fear, is much injured. I have deemed it best with Major Walker's approval to transfer, at once, a portion of those most exposed by water to the "Cornubia" so that proper steps may be taken to preserve them.

We have no facilities here, Twelve Carboys of Nitric Acid were thrown overboard, by order of the Captain, for the safety of the Ship.—

Smith Stansbury, Major.

Private and Unofficial.

[St. George's Ba.]
[September 14, 1863?]

Major Walker.

My faithful and efficient Clerk Mr. Gibson and myself toiled to get the "Ella and Annie" off with her precious Cargo.

If Captain Bonneau had taken the same interest, I am satisfied that his Steamer could have left a week earlier than she did, and escaped the Storm and consequent damage.

The "Ella and Annie" discharged her Cargo at Mrs. Todd's Wharf, and withdrew into the harbor—

Capt. B. declined to wharf his Steamer again into Mrs. Todd's Whf. to receive her cargo, and for reasons which I deemed frivolous.—

We had to load her by aid of the Schooner mentioned in another letter.

In the meantime Capt. B. beguiled his time in Hamilton 12 miles distant.

He says that he was sick, but if common report is to be credited, a woman who came over with him was the magnet, which distracted him from duty—

Smith Stansbury, Major.

St. George's Ba.
September 14th, 1863—

Capt. [Richard H.] Gayle, Steamer "Cornubia"

Captain—Please receive on board: 150 coils rope, 27 bales hammocks, 4 casks, 6 bales (cotton shirts), 8 bales white flannel shirts, 4 bales blue cloth great coats, 5 bales duck trousers, 33 bales duck frocks, 2 boxes combs, 2 casks tin pots.

Smith Stansbury, Major.
Per Geo. G. Gibson.

St. George's Ba.
September 16th, 1863

Robt. I. White, Esq., Richmond Arsenal.

My Dear Sir: I have received your letter of 8th Ulto: enclosing one from Mr. Robert White dated 5th, August, concerning the Omission to charge me with Requisition No. 235 for $267.62/100.

I enclose copy of my letter to Mr. Robert White.

To save trouble, I also enclose my check on Bank Cape Fear, Wilmington, in favor of E. C. Elmore Treasurer, for $267.62

This you will please hand in when entirely satisfied that I owe the money—otherwise return it to me—

The private matters referred to in your letter, I hope to reply to by the same Steamer which will convey this, but we are nearly all on the invalid list.

Major Walker is in bed with what is called the broken bone fever. Mr. Gibson is sick, Mr. Godet is sick and gone to Hamilton to recruit—

I can scarcely hold up my head, and have but one assistant, Mr. Allen. . . .

Smith Stansbury, Major.

St. George's Ba.
Sept. 17th, 1863—

Col. J. Gorgas.

Colonel: Referring to your letter of 7th, Inst. addressed to Major Huse, with instructions to purchase 5000 lbs. of Fish, or white Bonnet glue, for making Fuze Cases, and a Note to me, to purchase 2000 lbs. if to be had in Bermuda—None can be purchased here.—

The letter to Major Huse will be forwarded by the Steamer "Florida," which is expected to leave here on the 19th, and a copy by the Halifax Steamer expected to leave about 3rd October.—

Smith Stansbury, Major.

St. George's Ba.
September 17th, 1863

J. T. Bourne Esq.

Sir: I have received your letter of 16th, and note by Mr. Hawthorne, that in appointing Mr. Jos. Long Superintendent of Stevedores, he is not foreman as you term him—

I beg to refer you to Major N. S. Walker, who is clothed with plenary powers in all matters concerning the interests of the Confederate States in these Isles, and, with whose approbation the appointment was made—

Smith Stansbury, Major.

St. George's Ba.
September 19th, 1863—

Colonel J. Gorgas,
Enclosed please find List of Cargo Steamer "Phantom."

Smith Stansbury, Major.

P.S.—More powder would have been sent, but it was found that some slight coopering was needed to secure safety in the shipment of the balance at this particular place, and Captain Porter could not wait for it to be brought from the other powder ground.

St. George's Ba.
September 21st, 1863—

Colonel J. Gorgas.
Colonel: The Steamer "Cornubia" left this Port on the 18th, Instant for Wilmington. It is commonly reported, and believed that she was captured shortly after her departure by one of the enemy's cruisers, and seen in company with her. I however discredit the report, but will send by the next Steamer copies of all papers forwarded by the "Cornubia."

Smith Stansbury, Major.

St. George's Ba.
September 22nd, 1863—

Col. J. Gorgas.
Colonel: Referring to my letter of 12th Inst. in relation to Salaries of Clerks.

Major Walker has promised me to write to you, giving his views which accord with my own.

I earnestly recommend that I be allowed to pay Mr. George P. Black, and Mr. G. Alexandre $1000. per annum each. Further, that I be allowed to pay my chief clerk, not less than $1200. and I recommend $1500. I could not replace him by any ten men I could hire here, at Salaries of from $500. to $1000. each. In a private letter, I will endeavour to give you an idea of the cost of Board and Lodging in Bermuda, which I am satisfied that for want of full information you greatly underrate.

Smith Stansbury, Major.

St. George's Ba.
September 25th, 1863—

Colonel J. Gorgas.

Colonel: The Cargo of the "Coral Isle," of which you have Invoices has been landed and Stored in our principal Warehouse (Penno's).

We have just received Bills of Lading from Mess. S. Isaac Campbell and Co. of the following named vessels bound for this Port.—

"Rovers Bride" with 320 pigs lead, 510 boxes tin plates (Probably sheet tin).

"Glendower": 1731 pigs lead, 30 cases caps, 24 bales sulp. acid, 1 cask sling-hatchets, 186 bales rkt. paper (1802 reams), 46 bales, 66 bales ammuntn. paper (2850 reams), 50 bales white serge (1000 pieces) 10 casks wedge axes.

"Eitea," 800 boxes, marked, Charcoal and Coke.

These I happen to know, contain sheet tin, from shipping similar Packages—

Smith Stansbury, Major.

St. George's Ba.
October 1st, 1863—

Mr. John T. Bourne.

Sir: Please load the "Flora," (Mr. Campbell agrees to take some freight) with 250 Pigs Lead, 89 Packages from the "Harkaway," 50 Cases Shoes, 8 Boxes Flannels.

Smith Stansbury, Major.

St. George's Ba.

October 6th, 1863—

Capt. Bonneau, S. S. "Ella and Annie"—

Please send to Penno's Whf. at your convenience, advising me of the time, so that I may have a Custom's Officer in attendance, the 2 Cases Cavalry Equipments—18 Pigs Lead—Balance of Cargo on your Steamer.

Smith Stansbury, Major.

St. George's Ba.

October 8th, 1863—

Mr. John T. Bourne.

My dear Sir: The following is a list of Religious Books consigned to you by Mess Stringer Pembroke and Co. London per "Glendower," in the name of R. E. Terry.

—Boxes marked A. Testaments, Tracts, and Prayer Books.

—3 Boxes ....   "   "

These Books are for the Camps and Hospitals of the Confederate Army, and I am anxious, unless the number of Boxes is too great, to have them forwarded by the first opportunity, at any rate, a reasonable proportion—

Smith Stansbury, Major.

St. George's Ba.

October 16th, 1863.

Col. J. Gorgas.

Dear Sir: Your favor of 21st Ulto. in regard to forwarding Saltpetre, &c. has been received, and copy of your instructions have been handed to Major N. S. Walker who will give them due attention.

Smith Stansbury, Major.

P.S. Allow me to suggest that, as you frequently write several letters of the same date to one correspondent, it would be a good plan to number them, there would then be no difficulty in answering any particular letter, and it would also show which document was missing, in case of the loss or miscarriage of any particular letter. The above suggestion is from Mr. Black, and I shall adopt it in future myself.

St. George's Ba.
Oct. 20th, 1863—

Col. J. Gorgas.

Sir: Your official letter of the 28th Ulto. has been received, and contents duly noted. Your instructions will be followed out, and are now in a state of progress.

I will try to get ready to go over on the next trip of the "Cornubia" in about ten days—but fear I will be unable to do so; at any rate I will be able to leave on her succeeding trip.

Smith Stansbury, Major.

St. George's, Ba.
October 20th, 1863—

[Major N. S. Walker?]

Major: The Schooner "Ringwood" was hired as I understand by Mr. Bourne a Confederate Agent. If the bill rendered is according to the terms of a Contract made by him, I do not know how we can repudiate it, except upon the ground that he transcended his authority.

If the payment of the Bill by you depends upon my approval, I cannot give it, because I consider the charges extortionate.

Smith Stansbury, Major.

St. George's Oct. 23rd, 1863—

Col. J. Gorgas.

Col.: Enclosed please find List of Cargo and Bill of Lading S. S. "Ella and Annie." The Agent of the Steamer (Mr. Jervey) informs me that no Charter Party is necessary on this side, as an agreement has been made at the Port of Discharge.

Great difficulty is experienced in the adjustment of accounts by reason of the refusal on the part of Mr. Seixas to receipt for Stores brought by Private Steamers. Without these "distribution lists," we are wanting in the proper Subvouchers for the deliveries of Cargoes.

Smith Stansbury, Major.

St. George's Ba.
Oct. 23rd, 1863—

Mr. J. M. Seixas, Agt. of War Dept.

Sir: Enclosed please find List of Cargo and B/L S. S. "Ella and Annie" chartered by Government to go to Texas and released by Order of the War Dept. under an agreement to carry Government freight to Wilmington. As the charter was made on your side, you have, probably instructions as to rates of freight &c.

Smith Stansbury, Major.

P.S. I will be extremely obliged to you, if you will request returns of receipts in proper form for shipments by private Steamers from the various officers on duty at your Post, as without them I have no Subvouchers except the Bills of Lading.

St. George's Ba.
October 27th. 1863—

Mrs. Cecilia C. Todd.

Madam: Above is a copy of the only reply I have made to Mr. Gray's notes, which copy you requested. I find that I received no communication from you between the dates you mention viz. 14th & 27th July last—

I enclose "Triplicate" accounts for one quarter's rent due you.

Please sign one where I have ruled a pencil line, and return it to me, by the bearer.

By signing the other two and presenting them to Major N. S. Walker he will pay the amount.

Smith Stansbury, Major.

St. George's Ba.
November 2nd, 1863—

Mrs. Cecilia C. Todd.

Madam: Your note of 31st Ulto has been received.

I regret that a misunderstanding should exist in regard to the removal of the Crab.

Capt. Long informs me that it was done for your protection as he feared some injury might have been sustained by detached lumps of Coal, about being landed falling upon it.

It did not interfere at all with the erection of the stage.

I will execute a power of Attorney in favor of N. S. Walker Esq. by whom payments for rent &c. under agreement between us, made 27th Ulto: will be made, and, to whom I beg all communications may in future be addressed.

Smith Stansbury, Major.

Part II
Cargo Manifests

Editor's Note to Part II

As was explained in the Acknowledgments to this volume, the cargo manifests of the blockade runners plying between Bermuda and the Confederate States were located in the Custom House at St. George's, Bermuda. Mr. Hugh Miller and Mr. Harry Parker, of Hamilton, Bermuda, past and present Collectors of Customs, were most instrumental in finding and making available this material.

These manifests are interesting and important for a variety of reasons. They give a fairly complete picture of the type and quantity of supplies reaching the Confederacy—military and civilian alike. They indicate the character of the ships used as blockade runners, their tonnage, and the names of the blockade-running captains. From them a great deal may be learned of the South's fluctuating needs and of its efforts to supply these deficiencies. The difference in tonnage of ships bearing the same name is generally an indication that the original vessel was captured and another put into service under the same designation. Perhaps the most important thing about these manifests is what they show of the volume of commerce flowing through the Federal blockading squadrons.

Concerning the method used in editing these manifests for publication, it should be stated that it is not certain that all cargoes listed were destined for the South, since blockade runners, for obvious reasons, usually cleared for a neutral port. A careful sifting was made, to exclude those clearly going to Nassau or to some other unblocked port, and to include all those which were patently running the blockade, as well as all "border-line" cases. The introductory heading of each manifest is abbreviated and standardized to give all necessary information. The actual cargo lists, which appear in tabular form in the originals, are rearranged to conserve space.

Finally, cargo identification marks, which are fairly numerous in the originals, are omitted here since it seems that little use could be made of them. The meaning of some of these marks is selfevident, such as "OB" which, preceding an entry of a quantity of gunpowder, would obviously mean Ordnance Bureau. In the same way "ND" would be Navy Department and "MD" Medical Department. But the majority of the markings have as much meaning as Egyptian hieroglyphics, without some idea of the individuals and firms to which they refer. For example: S.S.S., JC&Co., JWC, SHC, LNB, YZ, and SBK, refer either to companies or individuals, and without some idea of marking codes of the various harbors, little can be made out of these ciphers.

Cargo Manifests

Bermuda, about 716 tons, St. George's for Nassau, April 22, 1862:

> From British ship *Ella,* Liverpool: 217 half chests tea, 120 bales bagging, 146 bales coffee, 180 coils rope, 5 bales twine.

Ella, about 887 tons, St. George's for Nassau, May 15, 1862, Carter, master:

> 8,072 sacks salt, 172 bolts bagging, 15 bales bagging, 69 coils rope, 120 bales gunny bagging.
>
> From *Herald:* 63 cases printing materials and stationery.

Minho, about 253 tons, St. George's for St. John's, N. B., September 26, 1862, F. T. Parke, master:

> From steamer *Phebe,* England: 48 hogsheads brandy, 21½ casks brandy, 63 cases brandy, 10 casks wine, 673 cases wine, 6¼ quarts whiskey, 14 hogsheads spirits, 8 cases apothecary ware, 1 case marine glasses, 1 case cutlery, 2 bales merchandise, 641 cases general merchandise, 7 cases quinine, 31 boxes candles, 5 cases drugs, 3 parcels thread, 8 packages merchandise (boots), 12 chests tea (from *Merrimac*), 1 case stationery, 12 cases mustard and starch, 37 barrels ale and porter, 6 barrels crushed sugar, 1 box sardines, 4 cases merchandise (meats), 14 kegs gunpowder, 2 cases merchandise, 5 cases tea, 1 case screws, 28 cases tin, 32 cases shoes.
>
> From *Gladiator,* Liverpool: 441 cases hardware, 83 cases merchandise, 4 cases merchandise.
>
> From *Merlin,* Halifax: 17 packages general merchandise, 500 bushels salt, 12 sacks salt, 7 rolls lead, 3 bags pepper, 10 bags coffee, 25 sheets iron, 3 cases cigars, 113 boxes soap.

Urana, about 260 tons, St. George's for Florida, October 20, 1862:

> 315 tons of coal, 7 shovels.

Herald, about 283 tons, St. George's for St. John's, N. B., October 25, 1862, L. M. Coxetter, master:

> From warehouse, imported per *Gladiator:* 30 cases quinine, 201 cases hardware, 101 cases general merchandise, 64 barrels combustible merchandise, 167 boxes combustible merchandise, 500 bags saltpeter, 500 barrels gunpowder.
>
> Transshipped from *Delta,* Halifax: 3 cases merchandise.
>
> From John T. Bourne's warehouse: 4 quarts brandy, 1 hogshead sherry wine.
>
> Transshipped from *Ella,* Liverpool: 1 case merchandise, 25 hams and

25 cheeses, 12 cases brandy.

52 bundles oakum, 42 cases and trunks consisting of boots, shoes, flannels, and general merchandise, £1,333.10.6.

Charles, about 43 tons, St. George's for Nassau, December 4, 1862, D. C. Rhodenwall, master:

160 half barrels gunpowder, 40 cases gunpowder, 3 cases cutlery, 190 cases tin.

Cornubia, about 259 tons, St. George's for Trinidad, B. W. I., December 12, 1862, J. Burroughs, master:

525 bales containing general merchandise from *Justitia,* London, 1 trunk, 1 case.

Evelina, about 44 tons, St. George's for Nassau, January 3, 1863, Higgs, master:

Transshipped from *Justitia,* London: 20 cases general merchandise, 26 cases general merchandise, 57 bales, 1 box samples.

Cornubia, about 259 tons, St. George's for Nassau, January 26, 1863, J. Burroughs, master:

Imported per *Justitia,* London: general merchandise, 157 bales, 260 cases, 1 cask, 100 pigs lead, 50 bundles steel rod.
Imported per *Merrimac:* 35 cases brandy.
Imported per *Harriet Pinckney:* 1 case merchandise, 1 cask brushes.

Harvest Queen, about 136 tons, St. George's for Matamoras, Mexico, February 24, 1863:

9 cases dry goods, 32 bales dry goods, 17 kegs nails, 4 boxes pickles, 8 boxes bay rum, 1 box wire, 24 brooms, 23 shovels, 16 boxes tobacco, 9 barrels ale, 6 kits salmon, 1 barrel cheese, 3 cases shoes, 20 boxes herrings, 26 bags hops, 60 boxes brandy, 4 barrels barley, 45 grindstones.

Cornubia, about 259 tons, St. George's for Nassau, February 25, 1863, J. Burroughs, master.

Imported per *Justitia,* London, value £10,000: 130 bales and 25 cases manufactured merchandise, 50 barrels saltpeter, 100 boxes tin, 100 pigs lead, 100 ingots tin.
Imported per *Gladiator,* value £4,500: 111 cases hardware, 72 boxes combustible merchandise, 178 boxes combustible merchandise.
Imported per *Delta:* 1 package wearing apparel.
Imported per *Miriam:* 1 case wearing apparel.
Imported per *Merrimac:* 600 barrels gunpowder.
4 cases stationery, £50.0.0, 45 cases brandy from John T. Bourne's warehouse.

Cornubia, about 259 tons, St. George's for Nassau, March 27, 1863, J. Burroughs, master.

Imported per *Justitia,* London: 122 cases manufactured merchandise, 42 casks hardware, 150 barrels saltpeter, 100 pigs lead, 100 ingots tin, 350 boxes cartridges.

5 bales merchandise.

From W. L. Penno's store, imported from London per *Gladiator:* 50 bales general merchandise.

Imported per *Dashing Wave:* 8 cases general merchandise, 250 cases hardware.

From Hunter's and Penno's warehouse, imported per *Phebe:* 200 cases brandy.

From John T. Bourne's warehouse, imported per *Merrimac,* London: 80 cases brandy.

6 packages merchandise, value £50.0.0.

General Beauregard, about 824 tons, St. George's for St. John's, N.B., April 7, 1863, L. M. Coxetter, master:

From W. L. Penno's warehouse, imported per *Gladiator,* Liverpool: 30 cases containing hardware, 521 bags saltpeter, 108 cases containing hardware.

From J. S. Hunter's warehouse, imported per *Phebe,* London: 285 cases containing hardware.

From A. J. Musson's warehouse, imported per *Miriam,* London: 68 cases manufactured merchandise.

From whale house, imported per *Justitia,* London: 310 boxes ammunition.

From John T. Bourne's warehouse, imported per *James,* London: 30 cases gin.

From John T. Fisher's warehouse, imported per *Delta,* Liverpool: 130 cases boots and shoes.

600 packages general merchandise, consisting of beef, pork, cloth, pease, flour, &c., £2,300.0.0.

From John T. Bourne's warehouse, imported per *Merrimac,* London: 25 cases brandy.

From same warehouse, imported per *Merlin,* Halifax: 1000 cigars.

3 hogsheads, 2 quarter casks, 8 demijohns, 1 jug brandy, 4 quarter casks and 19 cases wine, 40 barrels potatoes.

Merrimac, about 536 tons, St. George's for Nassau, April 17, 1863, Porter, master:

Part inboard cargo reported 5 September, 1862.

From W. L. Penno's warehouse, imported per *Dashing Wave:* 232 cases manufactured merchandise, 501 bales manufactured merchandise.

From W. L. Penno's warehouse, imported per *Gladiator* and *Phebe:*

2 boxes combustible merchandise, 2 cases hardware, 100 cases brandy
From warehouse, imported per *Merrimac:* 50 barrels powder.
From A. J. Musson's warehouse, imported per *Miriam:* 6 cases hardware.

Robert E. Lee, about 360 tons, St. George's for St. John's, N.B., April 24, 1863, Wilkinson, master:

From J. S. Hunter's warehouse, imported per *Harriet Pinckney,* London: 300 cases hardware, 300 boxes combustible merchandise.
From A. J. Musson's warehouse, imported per *Miriam,* London: 6 cases hardware.
From W. L. Penno's and John T. Bourne's warehouse, imported per *Merrimac,* London: 4 guns, 300 shell, 1 box fuses, 44 cases shoes, 5 bales merchandise, 23 cases brandy.
From W. L. Penno's warehouse, imported per *Gladiator:* 89 cases hardware.
From same warehouse, imported per *Phebe,* London: 200 cases brandy, 50 barrels saltpeter.
General merchandise: 6 kegs, 28 cases, 5 casks.
200 pigs lead, 70 ingots tin, 90 barrels beef and pork.
From warehouse: 7 quarter casks brandy, 195 gallons, 4 puncheons rum, 376 gallons, 1 quarter cask brandy, 28 gallons, 1 puncheon rum, 96 gallons.
From J. W. Musson's warehouse, imported per *Delta:* 10 demijohns gin, 20 gallons.
Imported per *Delta:* 40 demijohns and 25 cases gin.
Imported per *Merrimac:* 20 cases brandy.
55 cases general merchandise, value £1.263.5.1.

Cornubia, about 259 tons, St. George's for Nassau, May 8, 1863, Burroughs, master:

From W. L. Penno's warehouse, imported per *Gladiator,* Liverpool: 200 cases hardware, 250 boxes combustible ammunition.
From same warehouse, imported per *Justitia,* London: 25 bundles hardware, 151 barrels saltpeter, 50 pigs lead, 44 cases merchandise.
From same warehouse, imported per *Merrimac,* London: 133 packages hardware.
From same warehouse, imported per *Dashing Wave,* London: 15 cases hardware, 56 cases general merchandise.
From same warehouse, imported per *Phebe,* London: 200 cases brandy.
From John T. Bourne's warehouse, imported per *Merrimac,* London: 63 cases brandy.
From warehouse, imported per *Princess Royal:* 21 bundles telegraph wire.
Group of cargo, valued at £169.0.0: 37 barrels beef and pork, 34 boxes cheese, 5 barrels molasses, 16 sacks salt, 56 boxes harness.

Eugenie, about 239 tons, St. George's for Nassau, May 13, 1863, R. C. Halpin, master:

From A. J. Musson's warehouse, imported per *Miriam,* London: 154 cases hardware, 5 cases merchandise, 200 boxes combustible merchandise.

From Hunter's warehouse, imported per *Merrimac:* 50 cases hardware.

From W. L. Penno's warehouse, imported per *Gladiator:* 20 boxes combustible merchandise, 31 cases hardware.

From same warehouse, imported per *Justitia:* 100 pigs lead, 51 ingots tin, 120 cases general merchandise, 44 bales general merchandise.

From same warehouse, imported per *Phebe:* 100 cases brandy.

Imported per *Princess Royal,* New York: 29 coils telegraph wire.

From Penno's warehouse, imported per *Phebe,* London: 36 packages general merchandise.

64 barrels beef and pork, value £190.0.0.

Cornubia, about 259 tons, St. George's for Nassau, June 5, 1863, Burroughs, master:

From A. J. Musson's warehouse, imported per *Miriam:* 100 boxes combustible merchandise, 99 cases hardware.

101 boxes combustible ammunition.

From W. L. Penno's warehouse, imported per *Justitia,* London: 50 pigs lead, 41 bales general merchandise, 63 cases general merchandise, 25 bales general merchandise, 5 carboys acid.

From John T. Bourne's warehouse, imported per *Miriam,* London: 5 cases brandy.

3½ barrels borax, 30 coils telegraph wire, 100 barrels beef and pork, 40 boxes bacon, 76 barrels onions (9880 lbs.), 1 barrel potatoes.

R. E. Lee, about 360 tons, St. George's for Nassau, June 5, 1863, Wilkinson, master:

From J. S. Hunter's warehouse, imported per *Harriet Pinckney* and *Merrimac:* 389 cases hardware, 250 boxes combustible merchandise.

From same warehouse, imported per *Miriam,* London: 110 boxes combustible merchandise.

From W. L. Penno's warehouse, imported per *Justitia* and *Dashing Wave,* London: 65 cases hardware, 9 casks hardware, 12 cases general merchandise, 250 kegs lead, 157 cases brandy, 54 bales general merchandise.

From John T. Bourne's warehouse, imported per *Miriam,* London; 19 cases brandy.

Group cargo, valued at £1,300.0.0: 185 barrels beef and pork, 116 bags coffee, 10 cheese, 8 kegs butter, 2 cases blacking, 2 barrels kerosine oil.

2½ casks pale brandy, 197 barrels onions.

Eugenie, about 239 tons, St. George's for Nassau, June 11, 1863, Halpin, master:

> From W. L. Penno's warehouse, imported per *Gladiator,* Liverpool: 86 cases hardware.
>
> From same warehouse, imported per *Justitia* and *Dashing Wave,* London: 6 cases general merchandise, 100 bales general merchandise.
>
> From A. J. Musson's warehouse, imported per *Miriam:* 9 cases merchandise.
>
> 27 coils telegraph wire, 200 barrels beef and pork, 2 casks linseed oil, 78 barrels onions, 3 cases stationery.

Lord Clyde, about 457 tons, St. George's for Nassau, June 20, 1863, Joannes Wyllie, master:

> Inbound cargo, reported 15th instant.
>
> From John T. Bourne's warehouse, imported ·per *Harkaway,* Porto Rico: 100 bags coffee, 180 kegs rum, 69 boxes brandy.

Emma, about 191 tons, St. George's for Nassau, July 7, 1863, David Leslie, master:

> From W. L. Penno's warehouse, imported per *Justitia,* London: 27 cases manufactured merchandise, 25 casks hardware, 250 boxes hardware, 80 pigs lead, 100 ingots tin.
>
> From same warehouse, imported per *Dashing Wave:* 75 cases manufactured merchandise.
>
> From John T. Bourne's warehouse, imported per *Merrimac,* Liverpool: 30 cases brandy.
>
> Group merchandise, valued at £2,500.0.0: 46 barrels beef and pork, 347 bars iron, 10 bales hops, 89 packages general merchandise, 270 packages.

Lady Davis, about 259 tons, St. George's for Nassau, July 9, 1863, Richard H. Gayle, master:

> From Penno's warehouse, imported per *Harriet Pinckney,* London: 500 cases, 22 bales, 6 boxes, 4 barrels, 4 rolls general merchandise. 208 pigs lead.
>
> From John T. Bourne's warehouse, imported per *Merrimac:* 43 cases brandy.
>
> From same warehouse, imported per *Alpha,* Halifax: 2 cases merchandise.
>
> 190 barrels beef and pork, 5 rolls matting, 2 bales and 1 box bunting, 2 coils telegraph wire, 4 coils manilla rope.

Eugenie, about 239 tons, St. George's for Nassau, July 11, 1863, Joseph Fry, master:

> From W. L. Penno's warehouse, imported per *Harriet Pinckney,* London: 326 cases general merchandise, 50 bales general merchan-

dise, 1 roll leather, 3 casks hardware, 170 pigs lead, 9 cases acids.

From same warehouse, imported per *Dashing Wave*, London: 50 bales general merchandise.

From same warehouse, imported per *Justitia*, London: 50 boxes tin. Group merchandise, valued at £410.0.0: 28 barrels onions, 129 barrels beef and pork.

R. E. Lee, about 360 tons, St. George's for Nassau, July 22, 1863, Wilkinson, master:

From Penno's warehouse, imported per *Harriet Pinckney*, London: 329 cases, 156 bales, 63 boxes, 4 casks, 20 barrels, 1 keg general merchandise.

From same warehouse, imported per *Gladiator*, London: 28 cases hardware.

From same warehouse, imported per *Justitia*, London: 59 bundles hardware, 1 barrel saltpeter.

From Smith Island warehouse, imported per *Justitia:* 345 boxes cartridges.

From same warehouse, imported per *Dashing Wave*, London: 200 bales merchandise, 1 case steel.

From John T. Bourne's warehouse, imported per *Alpha*, Halifax: 7 trunks and 1 case merchandise.

From same warehouse, imported per *Eliza Barss:* 3 barrels bourbon whiskey, a bales nutgalls [?], 2 cases shoes. 5 cases brandy, ... pigs lead.

Transshipped from C.S.S. *Florida:* 21 chronometers, 4 sextants, 14 quadrants, 4 spy glasses, 7 bags coffee, 17 boxes tea, 25 boxes glass, 45 pairs boots.

From Gosling Brothers warehouse, imported: 20 boxes champagne, 12 barrels whiskey, 3 barrels oil.

Harkaway, about 59 tons, St. George's for Nassau, July 25, 1863, H. Frith, master:

From W. L. Penno's warehouse, imported per *Dashing Wave*, London: 43 bales calico and woolens, 51 trunks boots and shoes.

Banshee, about 216 tons, St. George's for Nassau, August 8, 1863, J. W. Steele, master:

From A. J. Musson's warehouse, imported per *Miriam*, London: 300 cases hardware, 300 boxes ammunition, 90 pigs lead.

From John T. Bourne's warehouse, imported per *Alpha*, Halifax: 2 cases merchandise.

Transshipped from *Florida*, Liverpool and Nassau: 40 coils rope, 2 bales bagging, 1 bag twine, 1 bale cotton wick, 10 bundles sacks, 2 firkins butter, 2 casks paint.

Transshipped from *Gibraltar*, Liverpool: 120 bales paper, 149 bundles shovels.

From C. Hunter's warehouse, imported per *Malicent:* 2 cases brandy.

Kent, about 59 tons, St. George's for Nassau, August 8, 1863, Theo. Perry, master:

Part inward cargo not landed: 15 barrels beef, 2 bales merchandise, 12 barrels port, 2 tierces hams.

Venus, about 365 tons, St. George's for Nassau, August 12, 1863, Charles Muney, master:

Transshipped from *Miriam:* 600 cases rifles.

From W. L. Penno's warehouse, imported per *Harriet Pinckney*, London: 300 boxes cartridges.

Transshipped from *Harriet Pinckney*, Halifax: 1 puncheon rum (100 gallons).

Cornubia, about 588 tons, St. George's for Nassau, August 13, 1863, Richard H. Gayle, master:

From W. L. Penno's warehouse, imported per *Harriet Pinckney*, Halifax: 50 coils rope.

From C. Hunter's warehouse, imported per *Harriet Pinckney*, London: 190 boxes cartridges.

50 boxes cartridges, 50 bales merchandise.

From W. L. Penno's warehouse, imported per *Harriet Pinckney*, London: 225 pigs lead, 218 boxes ammunition.

From C. Hunter's warehouse, imported per *Harriet Pinckney:* 226 cases rifles, 2 cases gun fittings.

From John T. Bourne's warehouse, imported per *James*, London: 1 case merchandise.

Eugenie, about 239 tons, St. George's for Nassau, August 13, 1863, Joseph Fry, commanding:

450 boxes cartridges, 140 cases rifles (Enfield), 68 bales blankets, 6 bales cartridge paper, 1 box merchandise (imported per *Alpha*), 1 box merchandise, 3 boxes bunting. Shipped by Major Smith Stansbury, C.S.A.

From *Malicent:* ¼ cask rum.

Ad. Vance [*Advance*], about 902 tons, St. George's for Nassau, August 14, 1863, Joannes Wyllie, master:

Transshipped from *Harkaway*, London: 287 packages merchandise, 100 boxes tin.

From C. Hunter's warehouse, imported per *Harriet Pinckney*, London: 50 boxes cartridges.

Transshipped from *Gibraltar*, Liverpool: 400 pigs lead.

From W. L. Penno's warehouse, imported per *Harriet Pinckney*, Halifax: 10 boxes candles, 101 bales gunny bagging, 8 coils rope, 1 case merchandise.

From same warehouse, imported per same ship, London: 121 cases merchandise, 16 barrels merchandise.

Elizabeth, about 676 tons, St. George's for Nassau, August 19, 1863, T. J. Lockwood, master:

From C. Hunter's warehouse, imported per *Harriet Pinckney*, England: 250 cases hardware, 23 cases hardware, 100 boxes ammunition.

Phantom, about 266 tons, St. George's for St. John's, N.B., August 19, 1863, S. G. Porter, master:

From W. L. Penno's warehouse, imported per *Harriet Pinckney*, London: 130 pieces pig iron, 402 cases cartridges, 20 cases steel, 100 ingots tin, 501 boxes sheet tin, 284 pigs lead, 100 bundles sheet iron. From A. J. Musson's warehouse, imported per *Miriam*, London: 97 cases rifles.

From *Florida*, Nassau: 45 bales bagging.

Alma, about 42 tons, St. George's for Nassau, August 20, 1863, D. C. Rhodenwall, master:

From *Florida*: 30 bags cotton waste, 35 casks paint, 2 cases merchandise, 2 packages merchandise.

Eugenie, about 239 tons, St. George's for Nassau, September 4, 1863, Joseph Fry, Master:

Transshipped from *Coral Isle*: 166 packages merchandise, 124 packages merchandise, 78 brass tubes, 168 bundles hardware.

From whale house, Tucker's Town, imported per *Phebe*, London: 300 bundles gunpowder.

From W. L. Penno's warehouse, imported per *Harriet Pinckney*, London: 2 hogsheads sugar.

R. E. Lee, about 360 tons, St. George's for Nassau, September 4, 1863, Wilkinson, master:

From John T. Bourne's warehouse, imported per *Merrimac*, London: 300 cases brandy.

From whale house, Smith Island, imported per *Merrimac*, London: 300 barrels gunpowder.

From same warehouse, imported per *Adela*, Liverpool, in 1862: 5 cases cartridges.

400 pigs lead, 22 bales army clothing, 25 bales army clothing, 9 bales medical stores, 10 cases medical stores, 10 tierces sugar, 150 boxes tin, 16 cases medical stores, 15 cases shoe thread, 60 bales, 13 cases

paper, 178 cases hardware, 20 cases hardware.
Imported per *Eliza Barss:* 5 cases drugs.
Imported in *Oleander:* 1 case merchandise.

Juno, about 259 tons, St. George's for Nassau, September 10, 1863, John A. Taylor, master:
From *Nebula:* 54 bales bagging.
20 pigs lead.

Hansa, about 250 tons, St. George's for Nassau, September 14, 1863, James E. Randle, master:
Imported per *Minstrel:* 122 packages dry goods.
Imported per *Nutfield:* 250 bags coffee.

Venus, about 365 tons, St. George's for Nassau, September 16, 1863, C. Murray, master:
From *Levant* and *Harkaway:* 50 barrels pork, 50 bags coffee, 10 barrels sugar, 122 packages merchandise.
60 boxes bacon.

Cornubia, about 588 tons, St. George's for Nassau, September 18, 1863, Richard H. Gayle, master:
From *Ella & Annie:* 200 cases rifles.
From Higgs and Hyland's warehouse, imported per *Harriet,* Nassau: 50 barrels alcohol.
From C. Hunter's warehouse, imported per *Liz Barnard:* 150 barrels pork.
From *Florida,* Nassau: 4 barrels white lead, 1 hogshead linseed oil.
545 coils rope, 6 casks general merchandise, 94 bales general merchandise, 2 boxes general merchandise.
From Musson's warehouse, imported per *Henrietta:* 15 casks brandy (401 gallons).
From same warehouse, imported per *Eagle:* 3 casks brandy (175 gallons).

Phantom, about 266 tons, St. George's for Nassau, September 19, 1863, S. G. Porter, master:
From *Resolution:* 9 cases whiskey, 2 cases gin.
1 case wine, 200 pigs lead, 2 Blakely guns, 50 cases leather, 50 cases Austrian rifles, 135 barrels pork, 150 barrels gunpowder, 1 case merchandise.

Flora, about 359 tons, St. George's for Nassau, October 2, 1863, Thomas Gillham, 1st officer, acting during illness of captain:
From Fisher's store, imported per *Nebula:* 25 cases sulphuric acid.

From *Nebula:* 100 cases of tea, 100 cases vegetable food, 40 casks saltpeter.

6 cases cotton cards, 250 pigs lead, 3 cases boots, 50 cases boots.

Dee, about 215 tons, St. George's for Nassau, October 3, 1863, G. H. Beir, master:

Inbound cargo reported September 28, less 1 package.

From Hunter's warehouse, imported per *Kestrie,* Nassau: 30 cases bacon.

From A. J. Musson's warehouse, imported per *Nutfield:* 100 bags coffee.

Julia, about .... tons, St. George's for Nassau, October 5, 1863, Jacob Stream, master :

From Higgs and Hyland's warehouse, imported per *Harriet,* Nassau: 6 barrels brandy, 20 cases brandy, 10 barrels gin, 50 cases gin, 19 barrels whiskey, 86 boxes schnapps, 48 boxes tin, 52 boxes pikes, 45 cases liquor, 22 cases merchandise, 45 cases bitters, 1 case nutmegs, 7 cases bonnets, 3 cases boots, 1 case spectacles, 3 cases whips, 1 case brushes, 1 case pins, 1 case pencils.

Advance, about 902 tons, St. George's for Nassau, October 6, 1863, Thomas M. Crossan, master:

From W. L. Penno' warehouse, imported per *Nebula,* London: 146 packages general merchandise.

From R. T. Davenport's warehouse, imported per *Harkaway:* 23 packages general merchandise.

From W. L. Penno's warehouse, imported per *Harriet Pinckney,* Halifax: 3 bags coffee, 2 casks merchandise, 1 barrel sugar, 1 trunk, 6 boxes merchandise.

From John T. Bourne's warehouse, imported per *James,* London: 1 trunk merchandise.

From Higgs and Hyland's warehouse, imported per *Tubal Cane:* 1 box wearing apparel, 2 boxes cotton cards.

77 bales gunny bagging, 46 coils manilla rope, 2 cases wine, 2 cases whiskey.

Alice, about 803 tons, St. George's for Nassau, October 16, 1863, J. Egan, master:

From Penno's warehouse, imported per *Nebula:* 2 kegs white lead, 2 kegs red lead, 1 drum boiled oil.

From Musson's warehouse: 129 coils rope, 23 bales bagging.

From Hunter's warehouse, imported per *Nutfield:* 150 half chests tea, 116 chests tea, 21 drums linseed oil, 58 drums linseed oil.

From Hunter's warehouse: 2 bales trawsumps [?], 35 bales blankets, 11 cases felt hats, 5 cases thread, 48 trunks shoes, 25 bales leather,

8 cases leather, 42 bundles leather, 29 bundles magnesia, 4 kegs cream tarter, 73 bags coffee, 3 bags coffee, 98 bags coffee, 1 bag coffee, 2 cases iod [?] potash, 5 cases calomel, 100 boxes soap, 15 cases mustard, 28 cases drugs, 2 drums drugs, 250 barrels salt meat, 1 case, 1 case, 2 cases, 3 cases, 1 case, 1 case, 2 cases, 1 case samples, 324 pigs lead.

Ella and Annie, about 905 tons, St. George's for Nassau, October 26, 1863, F. N. Bonneau, master:

From A. J. Musson's warehouse, and imported per *Miriam,* London: 203 [cases?] hardware, 1 case hardware.

Transshipped from *Glendower,* London: 150 pigs lead, 498 bags saltpeter, 10 barrels merchandise, 42 cases.

From Hunter's warehouse, imported per *Liz Barnard,* New York: 501 barrels beef and pork.

From Higgs and Hyland's warehouse, imported per *Harkaway,* London: 4 quarter casks brandy.

From W. L. Penno's warehouse, imported per *Harriet Pinckney,* Halifax: 481 sacks salt.

Aline, about 801 tons, St. George's for Nassau, October 28, 1863, E. A. Lagarde, master:

1057 tons coal.

Ella, about 124 tons, St. George's for Nassau [November 1, 1863?], Alexander E. Swasey, master:

From Higgs and Hyland's warehouse: 200 barrels beef and pork.

From W. L. Penno's warehouse, imported per *Harriet Pinckney,* London: 150 casks cavalry equipments, 1 case merchandise.

From *Glendower:* 300 sacks saltpeter.

From W. L. Penno's warehouse, imported per *Zygia,* London: 5 cases boots, 1 parcel boots, 201 bundles iron hoops, 1 bale bagging (value £10).

Flora, about 359 tons, St. George's for Nassau, November 2, 1863, George M. Horner, master:

From Penno's warehouse, imported per *Nebula:* 40 bales bagging.

From Fisher's warehouse, imported per *Nebula:* 23 cases sulphuric acid.

From Fisher's warehouse, imported per *Harkaway:* 8 bales of saddlery.

From Fisher's warehouse, imported per *Juno:* 2 cases silk handkerchiefs, 10 cases dry goods.

From Penno's warehouse, imported per *Zygia:* 200 bundles hoop iron.

From Hunter's warehouse, imported per *Lemuella:* 583 bundles shovels, 313 pigs lead.

From Trot and Atwood, 10 bags coffee.

Dee, about 215 tons, St. George's for Nassau [November 2, 1863?], G. H. Beir, master:

From R. T. Davenport's warehouse, imported per *Harkaway,* London: 99 boxes soap, 70 barrels sugar, 100 kegs soda, 10 barrels copperas, 104 bags coffee, 74 barrels pork, 15 casks oil, 1 cask emery paper, 5 casks machinery, 7 bales merchandise, 3 bales woolens, 2 bales woolens, 1 bale stationery, 1 bale canvas, 1 cask ink, 2 barrels hardware, 15 kegs lead.

From A. J. Musson's warehouse, imported per *Nutfield,* Nassau: 100 bags coffee.

From W. L. Penno's warehouse, imported per *Zygia:* 103 cases bacon.

From R. T. Davenport's warehouse, imported per *Milina:* 27 cases bacon.

Advance, about 902 tons, St. George's for Nassau, November 3, 1863, John J. Guthrie, master:

From W. L. Penno's warehouse, imported per *Rover's Bride:* 35 casks oil, 100 boxes tin plate, 4 cases merchandise, 85 bundles leather, 125 bales blankets, 1 case patterns, 4 cases merchandise, 12 cases merchandise, 23 cases merchandise.

From John T. Bourne's warehouse, imported per *James:* 4 cases merchandise, 5 cases leather, 2 cases shoes, 1 coil manilla rope.

From A. J. Musson's warehouse, imported per *Goodhue,* New York: 1 barrel brandy, 7 cases whiskey, 1 case brandy.

1 cask tallow, 2 casks oil.

Cornubia, about 588 tons, St. George's for Nassau, November 4, 1863, Richard H. Gayle, master:

From W. L. Penno's warehouse, imported per *Harriet Pinckney:* 58 cases bacon, 3 casks bacon, 19 hogsheads bacon, 3 cases cartridge paper, 1 case blankets.

From same warehouse, imported per *Rover's Bride:* 12 bales, 1 case.

From Hunter's warehouse, imported per *Glendower,* London: 15 cases caps, 36 pigs lead, 300 sacks saltpeter.

From A. J. Musson's warehouse, imported per *Miriam,* London: 64 cases rifles.

From Higgs and Hyland's warehouse, imported per *Harkaway:* 4 quarter casks brandy.

R. E. Lee, about 360 tons, St. George's for Nassau, November 4, 1863, John Knox, master:

From A. J. Musson's warehouse, imported per *Miriam,* London: 145 cases arms.

From W. L. Penno's stores, imported per *Harriet Pinckney:* 29 barrels pork, 1 box bacon, 372 pigs lead.

From C. Hunter's warehouse, imported per *Glendower,* London: 90

sacks saltpeter, 28 pigs lead.

Imported per *Magrettia* [?]: 160 sacks saltpeter.

From C. Todd's warehouse, imported per *Lemuella:* 8 packages merchandise.

Imported per *Goodhue,* New York: 1 case wire rope.

From A. J. Musson's warehouse, imported per *Goodhue,* New York: 2 barrels brandy.

From J. Peniston: 1 puncheon rum.

Ariosta, about 587 tons, St. George's for Nassau, November [23?], 1863, Alfred Patten, master:

1100 tons coal.

Hilja, about 568 tons, St. George's for Nassau, November 26, 1863, G. G. Bussell, master:

Part inward cargo reported.

Imported per *Cupid,* Halifax: 19 cases hardware.

Flora, about 359 tons, St. George's for Nassau, December 4, 1863, George M. Horner, master:

From Penno's store, imported per *Coral Isle:* 3 bales merchandise, 26 cases merchandise, 27 bales merchandise, 3 bales merchandise, 71 bundles shovels, 38 bundles spades, 9 bundles shovels, 5 bundles handles, 2 cases merchandise, 2 cases merchandise, 15 cases merchandise, 2 cases merchandise.

Prom Penno's store, imported per *Elia:* 200 sacks saltpeter.

From Johnson's warehouse: 189 cases merchandise.

From Fisher's warehouse, imported per *Juno:* 1 case merchandise, 2 cases brandy.

From same warehouse, imported per *Nebula:* 10 kegs white lead, 5 drums oil.

From Johnson's warehouse, imported per *Josephine:* 1 case ale.

From W. P. Campbell: 1 case haberdashery, 1 bundle clothing, 1 trunk clothing, 1 trunk clothing.

Coquette, about 391 tons, St. George's for Nassau, December [13?], 1863, R. R. Carter, master:

From John T. Bourne's warehouse, imported per *Liz Barnard:* 45 barrels pork, 256 barrels pork.

From Todd's warehouse, imported per *Goodhue:* 4 casks insulators, 3 casks telegraph wire, 60 bundles telegraph wire.

From Todd's warehouse, imported per *Lemuella:* 14 cases railroad caps.

From Hunter's warehouse, imported per *Estea:* 300 sacks saltpeter.

From same warehouse, imported per *Glendower:* 100 pigs lead.

From purchase account: 30 barrels pork.

From Penno's warehouse, imported per *Zanipa:* 2 cases woolens.

From *Coquette:* 2 packages.

From Penno's warehouse, imported per *Dashing Wave:* 8 cases steel.

Inward cargo from Liverpool.

Heroine, about 108 tons, St. George's for Nassau, December [13?] 1863, D. J. Page, master:

From W. L. Penno's warehouse, imported per *Coral Isle:* 61 cases shoes, 85 casks cavalry equipments.

From same warehouse, imported per *Harriet Pinckney:* 1 case phosphorus.

From Hunter's warehouse, imported per *Estea:* 100 sacks saltpeter.

From same warehouse, imported per *Glendower:* 200 pigs lead.

From John T. Bourne's warehouse, imported per *James,* London: 13 cases boots and shoes.

Ranger, about 350 tons, St. George's for Nassau, December [18?], 1863, John T. Holmes, master:

From Penno's store, imported per *Nebula:* 30 barrels copperas, 60 barrels loaf sugar, 50 caddies tea, 30 half chests tea.

From Fisher's warehouse, imported per *Nebula:* 19 barrels salts, 20 kegs soda.

From same warehouse, imported per *Juno:* 2 cases brandy.

From Johnson's warehouse, imported per *Josephine:* 1 case quinine.

Imported per *Wild Hunter:* 1 case merchandise.

200 sacks saltpeter, 200 cases rifles, 202 coils rope, 5 bales bagging, 19 barrels bagging, 50 bales rope, 106 cases engineer instruments, 3 cases sheet copper, 50 pigs lead, 1 case borax, 3 cases hand cards, 3 cases hand cards, 9 cases, 4 cases cotton cards, 20 drums oil.

Dair, about 179 tons, St. George's for Nassau, January 2, 1864, Thomas P. Skinner, master:

From Johnson's warehouse, imported per *Josephine:* 40 cases merchandise, 26 cases merchandise, 5 cases merchandise, 1 case merchandise, 1 case ale.

Imported per *Wild Hunter,* duty paid: 1 case merchandise.

From Penno's warehouse, imported per *Nebula:* 1 keg arsenic.

65 cases soda, 55 packages merchandise, 3 kegs merchandise, 4 bales, 1 bale bagging, 50 coils rope, 6 boxes herrings, 1 box whiskey, 2 boxes sugar, 2 cases merchandise, 25 packages merchandise, 1 bale merchandise, 4 bales merchandise.

From Penno's warehouse, imported per *Kohinor:* 10 cases.

Vesta, about 262 tons, St. George's for Nassau, January [3?], 1864, J. V. Eustice, master.

Imported per *Alpha,* Halifax: 2 cases merchandise.

From W. L. Penno's warehouse, imported per *Tampa,* Liverpool: 2 cases books.

Imported per *Josephine*, Liverpool: 3 cases beer.

From Higgs and Hyland's warehouse, imported per *Harkaway*, Liverpool: 2 cases merchandise.

From C. Hunter's warehouse, imported per *Kestrel:* 116 boxes bacon.

From John T. Bourne's warehouse, imported per *Goodhue*, New York: 3 cases whiskey.

Presto, about 164 tons, St. George's for Nassau, January 4, 1864, Wilkinson, master:

From Penno's warehouse, imported per *Nebula:* 2 kegs arsenic, 1 case tea, 6 barrels sugar, 2 drums oils, 1 drum turps.

From Fisher's warehouse, imported per *Juno:* 1 case merchandise, 6 cases brandy.

From same warehouse, imported per *Nebula:* 6 kegs black paint.

From R. Musson and Company: 1 case merchandise.

Imported per *Wild Hunter*, duty paid: 2 cases merchandise, 1 case merchandise, 1 cask wire.

From Johnson's warehouse, imported per *Josephine:* 13 cases merchandise, 29 cases merchandise.

Transshipment from *Alpha:* 19 cases merchandise.

Imported per *Arbutus:* 16 dozen [cases ?] ale.

Imported per *Nebula:* 8 kegs paint.

5 cases merchandise, 1 barrel whiskey, 1 barrel brandy, 2 trunks merchandise, 1 case merchandise.

Advance, about 902 tons, St. George's for Nassau, January 11, 1864, Thomas M. Crossan, master:

From C. Hunter's warehouse, imported per *Arbutus:* 17 cases general manufactured merchandise.

From W. L. Penno's warehouse, imported per *Jane Smith:* 69 bales, 80 cases general manufactured merchandise.

Harvest Queen, about 136 tons, St. George's for Nassau, January 12, 1864, H. H. Hollis, master:

From A. J. Musson's stores, imported per *Goodhue:* 25 boxes soap, 2 windsor soap, 39 boxes candles, 43 barrels vinegar, 90 bales oakum.

From Higgs and Hyland's stores, imported per *Harvest Queen* and *Oleander:* 800 coils rope, 429 cases whiskey, 33 eight casks brandy, 1 wood press.

From Penno's store, imported per *Kohinor:* 95 cases merchandise.

Nina, about 205 tons, St. George's for Nassau, January 14, 1864, George Squires, master:

Part of inward cargo not landed in Bermuda: 600 boxes bacon.

City of Petersburg, about 426 tons, St. George's for St. John's, N.B., January 15, 1864, F. W. Fuller, master:

> From C. Hunter's warehouse: 400 pigs lead, 215 barrels provisions, 3 cases copper, 10 barrels alcohol, 5 cases brass, 10 casks oil, 10 bundles springs, 4 tyres, 10 cases acid, 200 sacks saltpeter, 36 bundles steel.
>
> From Higgs and Hyland's warehouse: 10 bales gunny cloth, 19 coils rope, 1 barrel whiting, 2 barrels lard oil, 6 packages merchandise.

Nutfield, about 402 tons, St. George's for Nassau, January 29, 1864, Lawrence Marshall, master:

> From *Colombo,* imported per *Arbutus:* 29 bales merchandise.
>
> From Penno's warehouse, imported per *Nebula:* 49 bundles iron.
>
> From Johnson's warehouse, imported per *Josephine:* 19 packages merchandise.
>
> From N. S. Walker: 200 sacks saltpeter, 42 cases rifles, 19 cases leather, 50 cases soap.
>
> 300 pigs lead, 238 pigs lead, 10 bottles, 4 rolls lead, 1 cask wire, 2 casks wire, 4 casks wire, 5 casks zinc, 5 casks steel, 5 casks steel, 8 casks files, 11 barrels steel, 9 barrels twine, 2 casks merchandise, 2 casks merchandise, 13 casks axes, 8 brass guns, 23 bales blankets, 11 bales merchandise, 243 bales merchandise, 4 bales merchandise, 4 cases soap, 12 cases leather, 12 cases leather, 6 cases rifles, 11 cases rifles, 1 case rifles, 3 cases rifles, 9 cases leather, 2 cases merchandise, 30 bales bagging, 14 cases merchandise, 146 cases merchandise, 6 bundles shovels, 5 cases merchandise, 5 cases bits, 5 barrels, 1 keg, 18 cases, 15 cases.
>
> From Johnson's warehouse, imported per *Arbutus:* 6 cases ale.
>
> From Johnson's warehouse, imported per *Margaret,* duty paid: 43 bags bread, 1 roll wire, 1 box files.

Index, about 363 tons, St. George's for Nassau, February 2, 1864, George M. Horner, master:

> From Major N. S. Walker: 600 boxes cartridges, 147 sacks saltpeter, 52 coils rope, 5 cases leather, 7 cases leather, 29 cases leather, 2 cases canteens, 2 cases stationery, 1 case oil cans, 2 cases bayonets, 30 cases rifles, 14 cases carbines, 1 bale leather, 2 bales merchandise.
>
> From *Colombo,* imported per *Arbutus:* 28 packages merchandise.
>
> From Johnson's warehouse, imported per *Josephine:* 18 packages merchandise.
>
> From Johnson's warehouse: 6 cases.
>
> From Penno's warehouse, imported per *Nebula:* 40 bundles sheet iron.

Emily, about 253 tons, St. George's for Nassau, February [3?], 1864, Robert C. Halpin, master:

> From Todd's warehouse, imported per *Coral Isle*, London: 400 pigs lead, 50 kegs merchandise, 37 casks merchandise, 409 barrels merchandise, 2 bales merchandise, 1 case merchandise, 100 bundles merchandise.
> From Todd's warehouse: 515 sacks saltpeter, 12 cases whiskey. Value £15,000.

Caledonia, about 115 tons, St. George's for Nassau, February 6, 1864, N. P. Dutton, master:

> From Penno's store: 29 boxes bacon, 20 sacks saltpeter, 100 pigs lead.

Will O' The Wisp, about 117 tons, St. George's for Nassau, February 13, 1864, O. Capper, master:

> From Johnson's warehouse, imported per *Josephine:* 8 cases merchandise, 6 cases merchandise.
> From John T. Bourne: 28 cases merchandise.
> 60 cases bacon, 55 coils rope, 123 cases merchandise.

Advance, about 902 tons, St. George's for Nassau, February 13, 1864, John J. Guthrie, master:

> From Penno's warehouse: 30 bales leather, 13 bales cloth, 15 cases paper, 7 cases merchandise.
> From Skinner's warehouse, imported per *Nina:* 244 bales merchandise.
> From W. P. Campbell: 2 cases merchandise, 1 box merchandise, 1 chest tea, 2 half barrels merchandise, 1 keg butter, 1 box merchandise.
> From Johnson's warehouse, imported per *Josephine:* 5 cases caps, 270 cases books.
> From same warehouse, imported per *Aurora:* 1 trunk dry goods.

Hansa, about 257 tons, St. George's for Nassau, February 26, 1864, T. Atkinson, master:

> From Penno's store, imported per *Rover's Bride:* 8 packages merchandise.
> From same store, imported per *Jane Smith:* 7 packages merchandise, 102 pigs lead.
> From same store, imported per *Hansa:* 1 package merchandise.
> From Hunter's store, imported per *Arbutus:* 14 packages merchandise.
> From same store, imported per *Nina:* 14 coils rope.
> From Johnson's store, imported per *Josephine:* 94 packages merchandise, 15 packages merchandise.

City of Petersburg, about 426 tons, St. George's for St. John's, N.B., February 29, 1864, F. W. Fuller, master:

Shipped by Major N. S. Walker, from F. A. Hunter's warehouse: 8 tyres, 135 sacks saltpeter, 100 cases, 15 cases paper, 3 packages lead.

Stores: 13 cases champagne, 1 case whiskey, 1 case sherry, 1 barrel whiskey, 1 puncheon rum, 11 cases gin.

32 cases merchandise.

Florie, about 215 tons, St. George's for Nassau, March 1, 1864, T. Eyre, master:

Major Smith Stansbury: 1 black trunk, 3 small boxes.

From Heyl's, Hamilton, Bermuda: 8 boxes provisions (£50.0.0), 6 boxes merchandise, 1 cask, 4 boxes provisions.

From Lemmon and Company: 1 keg merchandise, 1 drum merchandise, 1 keg merchandise, 1 case merchandise, 8 cases merchandise.

From W. C. Dunham and P. C. Williams: 6 cases merchandise, 2 cases merchandise (£260.0.0).

From P. C. Williams: 3 cases merchandise, 6 bales merchandise.

From Penno's wharf: 124 boxes bacon.

Index, about 362 tons, St. George's for Nassau, March 1, 1864, George Henry, master:

From Fisher's warehouse, imported per *Juno:* 15 cases brandy.

From Johnson's warehouse, imported per *Arbutus:* 20 cases ale.

From Hunter's warehouse, imported per *Glendower:* 206 sacks saltpeter.

Imported per *Agrippina:* 600 boxes cartridges, 29 cases tools, 28 bales bagging, 4 cases [word illegible].

From purchase account, £600.0.0: 35 packages merchandise.

6 cases rifles, 2 cases carbines, 50 cases rifles, 4 bales leather, 29 cases leather, 4 cases merchandise, 1 case brass rivets, 28 cases stationery.

Coquette, about 391 tons, St. George's for Nassau, March 2, 1864, R. R. Carter, master:

From Johnson and Croft's warehouse, imported per *Josephine:* 9 cases merchandise, 2 drums merchandise, 1 cask merchandise, 4 cases merchandise.

From C. Hunter's warehouse, imported per *Arbutus:* 1 case.

Imported per *Harriet Pinckney:* 4 cases merchandise, 2 bales merchandise.

Imported per *Agrippina:* 1 barrel.

Thistle, about 305 tons, St. George's for Nassau, March 5, 1864, Alexander Hora, master:

From R. T. Davenport's warehouse: 12 packages merchandise, 20 cases merchandise.

From John T. Bourne's warehouse: 2 cases hardware.

From W. L. Penno's warehouse: 11 cases merchandise.

From C. Hunter's warehouse: 53 packages merchandise, 27 bundles rope, 5 bales bagging, 360 barrels pork, 50 sacks saltpeter, 115 boxes bacon, 2 barrels bacon.

Enterprise, about 627 tons, St. George's for Nassau, March 7, 1864, F. B. Phillips, master:

Coals, inward cargo.

Agrippina, about 275 tons, St. George's for Nassau, March 23, 1864, Alexander McQueen, master:

From John T. Bourne's warehouse, imported per *Lizzie Barnard:* 650 barrels provisions.

From Mrs. Todd's warehouse, imported per *Lemuella:* lot of lead as ballast.

100½ tons coal.

Elva, about 61 tons, St. George's for Nassau, March 24, 1864, James W. Culmer, master:

15 tierces beef (£60.0.0), 37 barrels beef (£76.0.0), 12 barrels beef (£39.10.0), 50 barrels potatoes (£25.0.0), 6 bags coffee (620 pounds, £22.4.0).

Advance, about 902 tons, St. George's for Nassau, March 26, 1864, Joannes Wyllie, master:

From Higgs and Hyland's store, imported per *Carl Emil:* 71 cases merchandise, 21 cases merchandise, 2 casks merchandise.

From Penno's store, imported per *Rover's Bride* and *Jane Smith:* 32 cases merchandise, 7 drums merchandise, 108 pigs lead.

From Johnson's warehouse, imported per *Nina:* 58 cases merchandise.

From same warehouse, imported per *Mathilde:* 2 cases merchandise.

From Hunter's store, imported per *Arbutus:* 31 bales merchandise.

From Hamilton, Bermuda: 3 hogsheads sugar, 50 coils rope.

1 trunk merchandise, 2 cases merchandise.

Minnie, about 253 tons, St. George's for Nassau, March 26, 1864, Thomas S. Gilpin, master:

From Hunter's warehouse, imported per *Glendower:* 440 pigs lead, 150 sacks saltpeter.

From same warehouse, imported per *Kestrel:* 279 boxes bacon.

North Heath, about 343 tons, St. George's for Nassau, March 29, 1864, John Burroughs, master:

Imported per *Harriet Pinckney*, London: 317 cases, 616 bags, general manufactured goods. 205 cases of the above value £4,100 for drawback.

Index, about 363 tons, St. George's for Nassau, March 29, 1864, Lawrence Marshall, master:

> From Johnson's warehouse, imported per *Nutfield:* 10 barrels flour, 4 barrels beef, 6 barrels pork.
> From same warehouse, imported per *Arbutus:* 12 cases brandy.
> From Fisher's warehouse, imported per *Juno:* 7 cases brandy.
> From *Colombo,* imported per *Arbutus:* 4 kegs white lead, 15 drums engine [?] oil.
> 250 cases rifles, 50 cases carbines. Duty paid, value £6,000. £120.0.0.
> 250 sacks saltpeter, 200 pigs lead, 10 cases steel, 8 cases acids, 1 case merchandise, 4 cases bunting, 1 case merchandise, 8 barrels medicines, 3 barrels sugar, 3 kegs medicines, 1 case medicines, 1 case merchandise.

Grey Hound, about 296 tons, St. George's for Nassau, March 29, 1864, George Henry, master:

> From Johnson and Croft's warehouse: 353 boxes bacon.
> From Todd's warehouse: 62 boxes bacon, 5 casks bacon.
> From Higgs and Hyland's warehouse: 64 bales merchandise, 15 bales leather, 113 cases and trunks merchandise, 1 cask merchandise, 51 trunks merchandise, 155 packages merchandise, 13 packages merchandise.
> Imported per *Mathilde:* 136 packages merchandise.

Edith, about 239 tons, St. George's for Nassau, April 9, 1864, Josiah Gregory, master:

> From Hunter's warehouse: 100 sacks saltpeter, 8 crates tarpaulin.
> From warehouse: 12 bales manilla rope.

Minnie, about 253 tons, St. George's for Nassau, April 26, 1864, Thomas S. Gilpin, master:

> From Hunter's warehouse, imported per *Harriet Pinckney:* 150 sacks saltpeter.
> From W. L. Penno's warehouse, imported per *Coral Isle:* 200 pigs lead.
> From Higgs and Hyland's warehouse: 137 barrels merchandise, 10 casks merchandise.
> From Todd's warehouse, imported per *Goodhue,* New York: 10 coils wire.
> From E. B. Todd's warehouse, imported per *Agrippina:* 243 cases merchandise.

Helen, about 342 tons, St. George's for Nassau, April 26, 1864, David Leslie, master:

> Transferred from *Remneys,* Liverpool: 101 cases merchandise, 105 bales merchandise.

Transferred from *North Heath:* 278 cases merchandise, 402 sacks saltpeter.

In transit: 20 tons iron.

Atalanta, about 253 tons, St. George's for Nassau, April 28, 1864, George M. Horner, master:

From Penno's warehouse: 145 boxes bacon, 61 casks bacon.

Imported per *Remneys:* 30 bales.

From Johnson's warehouse, imported per *Remneys:* 1 bale, 10 cases boots.

Imported per *Bonnie Belle:* 5 kegs horseshoe nails.

From Johnson and Croft's warehouse, imported per *Finnie's Drake* [?]: 1 case merchandise.

1 keg horseshoe nails, 1 box, 2 trunks, 2 bundles, 1 ton hoop iron.

Nonsuch, about 310 tons, St. George's for Matamoras, Mexico, April 29, 1864, George G. Strickland, master:

Transshipped from *Ella:* 53 barrels herrings.

From warehouse: 190 barrels flour, 749 bags corn, 20 tierces lard, 15 firkins butter, 10 cases butter, 100 boxes candles, 106 cases brandy, 558 packages merchandise.

Pevensey, about 455 tons, St. George's for Nassau, May 6, 1864, John Burroughs, master:

Imported per *Harriet Pinckney:* 36 cases rifles, 61 cases rifles, 24 cases rifles, 79 cases rifles, 12 cases carbines, 14 cases carbines, 17 cases sabers, 10 cases harness, 1 case harness, 200 sacks saltpeter, 60 cases medical stores.

Imported per *Coral Isle:* 3 barrels emery, 20 cases leather, 200 pigs lead.

Per purchase account: 6 cases steel, 4 barrels sugar, 10 cases acids, 10 cases stationery, 25 cases dry goods.

Imported per *Queen of Britain:* 8 bales grey woolens, 113 cases merchandise.

Imported per *Princess Royal:* 130 cases merchandise.

Imported per *Bonnie Belle:* 30 bluchers.

Imported per *Nutfield:* 2 casks beef, 2 casks pork.

Imported per *Goodhue:* 79 coils rope.

6 casks screws, 1 case emery paper, 9 cases steel, 5 boxes pistol [ammunition ?], 1 case merchandise.

Ecke, about 388 tons, St. George's for Nassau, May 7, 1864, John Prouings, master:

509 tons coal.

Index, about 362 tons, St. George's for Nassau, May 7, 1864, Lawrence Marshall, master.

> From Hunter's warehouse, imported per *Harriet Pinckney:* 100 bags saltpeter, 33 cases pistols.
>
> From Penno's warehouse, imported per *Coral Isle:* 26 cases leather, 2 cases shirt backs, 2 cases caps, 2 cases emery, 7 cases medical stores, 1 case medical stores, 2 cases screws.
>
> From Todd's warehouse, imported per *Lemuella:* 20 cases papa [?].
>
> From same warehouse, imported per *Justitia:* 15 cases medical stores.
>
> From Hunter's warehouse, imported per *Bonnie Belle:* 25 cases shoes.
>
> From Penno's warehouse, imported per *Justitia:* 5 cases steel.
>
> From Fisher's stores, imported per *Wild Hunter:* 1 case sheepskins, 1 keg wine, 1 keg wine.
>
> From Higgs and Hyland's warehouse, imported per *Carl Emil:* 20 bundles hoop iron.
>
> From Penno's warehouse, imported per *Nebula:* 100 bundles sheet iron.
>
> Duty paid on: 100 cases rifles, 50 cases carbines.
>
> 200 pigs lead.

Georgiana McCan, about 373 tons, St. George's for Nassau, May 11, 1864, George H. Corbett, master:

> Inboard cargo, reported May 6.
>
> 49 barrels onions (3770 pounds).

Atalanta, about 253 tons, St. George's for Nassau, May 23, 1864, George M. Horner, master:

> From Penno's and Brown's warehouse: 36 casks bacon, 308 boxes bacon.
>
> From Musson's warehouse, duty paid April 22: 3 bales gunny cloth, 30 bales merchandise, 3 coils rope, 311 bundles iron hoops.
>
> 400 barrels onions (32,000 pounds), 1 case merchandise, 2 iron standards, 1 coil wire rope, 1 chain, 1 wheel.

Mary Celestia, about 207 tons, St. George's for Nassau, May 23, 1864, M. P. Usina, master:

> Duty paid November 19, 1863: 5 cases merchandise, 6 bales merchandise.
>
> 21 cases shell, 77 bales blankets and blue cloth, 1 case merchandise, 2 bales merchandise, 39 casks bacon, 137 barrels pork, 1 box medicine, 2 cases merchandise, 1 trunk, 3 cases, 4 cases brandy.

Lynx, about 233 tons, St. George's for Nassau, May 23, 1864, P. C. Reid, master:

> From Todd's warehouse, imported per *Greyhound:* 431 packages machinery and hardware.

From same warehouse, imported per *Lemuella:* 62 packages merchandise.

From Hunter's warehouse, imported per *Bonnie Belle:* 47 packages merchandise.

Caledonia, about 115 tons, St. George's for Nassau, May 25, 1864, Charles Nelson, master:

47 boxes bacon, 28 casks bacon, 36 cases leather goods, 3 cases medical stores, 1 case merchandise.

Siren, about 20 tons, St. George's for Nassau, May 30, 1864, J. Peniston, master:

From Johnson's warehouse: 150 bundles hoop iron.

From James W. Musson's warehouse: 1 cask whiskey.

From N. C. McCallan's warehouse, 1 cask whiskey.

Duty paid on: 34 packages merchandise (value £1,000).

Helen, about 342 tons, St. George's for Nassau, May 28, 1864, David Leslie, master:

From Hunter's and Todd's warehouse: 61 bales merchandise, 23 cases merchandise, 4 boxes merchandise.

From Penno's warehouse: 170 pigs lead.

Imported per *Harriet Pinckney,* and duty paid on value £3,160—@ 2% £63.4.0: 30 cases carbines, 21 cases rifles, 50 cases rifles, 29 cases rifles, 28 cases sabers.

2 casks hatchets, 106 barrels pork, 7 boxes bacon, 2 cases merchandise, 2 cases merchandise, 20 barrels coffee, 13 bags coffee.

Lilian, about 246 tons, St. George's for Nassau, June 1, 1864, J. N. Maffit, master:

From Hunter's warehouse, imported per *Harriet Pinckney:* 300 sacks saltpeter, 1 case merchandise, 4 tierces sugar.

From Hunter's warehouse, imported per *Coral Isle:* 63 pigs lead, 28 packages hardware.

From same warehouse, imported per *Bonnie Belle:* 67 packages merchandise.

From same warehouse, imported per *Princess Royal:* 11 packages merchandise.

From same warehouse, imported per *Harkaway:* 15 packages merchandise.

From Penno's warehouse, imported per *Aurora:* 14 bales cloth.

Imported per *Harriet Pinckney,* value £4,880.2. paid £97.12. duty paid: 246 cases merchandise.

From John T. Bourne's warehouse, imported per *Nepha:* 2 cases merchandise.

From Higgs and Hyland's warehouse: 4 cases merchandise.

Imported per *Harkaway:* 6 cases merchandise.
Transshipped from *Delta,* Halifax: 1 case quinine.
From John T. Bourne's warehouse: 5 bales gunny cloth.
Duty paid on: 17 cases merchandise, 4 cases merchandise.

Florie, about 215 tons, St. George's for Nassau, June 1, 1864, Jesse De Horsey, master:

From Hunter's warehouse, imported per *Harriet Pinckney:* 200 sacks saltpeter.
From same warehouse, imported per *Estea:* 100 boxes tin.
From Penno's store, imported per *Coral Isle:* 137 pigs lead.
From Hunter's warehouse, imported per *Princess Royal:* 4 cases shoes, 19 bales blankets, 4 bales blankets.
Imported per *Bonnie Belle:* 33 bales merchandise, 2 cases merchandise, 23 cases shoes.
Imported per *Justitia:* 2 cases merchandise, 10 bales merchandise.
Imported per *Harriet Pinckney:* 3 tierces sugar, 11 cases caps (copper).
Imported per *Coral Isle:* 25 cases hardware, 79 sheets brass, 8 kegs hardware, 20 bales paper.
From W. L. Penno's warehouse, imported per *Jane Smith,* London, in August, 1863: 40 packages merchandise, 5 packages merchandise (duty paid).
From John T. Bourne's warehouse, imported per *Bonnie Belle:* 6 bales gunny bagging.
1 bale marchandise, 5 packages merchandise.

Pevensey, about 455 tons, St. George's for Nassau, June [3?], 1864, F. W. Crispin, master:

From Fisher's warehouse, imported per *Flora:* 16 cases boots.
From same warehouse, imported per *Juno:* 13 cases boots, 1 box hats, 2 cases chemicals.
From same warehouse, imported per *Nebula:* 206 cases tea, 2 cases chemicals.
From same warehouse, imported per *Harkaway:* 20 casks soda ash, 50 kegs soda, 3 casks salts.
From same warehouse, imported per *Pevensey:* 4 boxes whiskey.
From Penno's warehouse, imported per *Nebula:* 185 bundles sheet iron.
From Hunter's warehouse, imported per *Harriet Pinckney:* 316 sacks saltpeter.
From Penno's warehouse, imported per *Coral Isle:* 200 pigs lead.
Imported per *Colombo:* 130 boxes bacon.
Imported per *Harkaway:* 108 cases shoes, 8 bales woolens.
From Hunter's warehouse, imported per *Princess Royal:* 11 bales woolens, 9 cases shoes, 1 box stockings.
From same warehouse, imported per *Delta:* 5 cases hardware, 1 bag hardware.

From same warehouse, imported per *Alpha:* 2 boxes merchandise.
From same warehouse, imported per *Honesta:* 1 box merchandise.
From Todd's warehouse, imported per *Princess Royal:* 1 box merchandise, 1 box merchandise.
From Musson's warehouse, imported per *Josephine:* 9 boxes ale.
From same warehouse, imported per *Arbutus:* 10 boxes brandy.
Imported per *Rouen:* 10 boxes brandy, 5 boxes wine.

Lynx, about 233 tons, St. George's for Nassau, June 8, 1864, P. C. Reid, master:

From Penno's warehouse, imported per *Coral Isle:* 152 packages merchandise.
From Hunter's warehouse, imported per *Harriet Pinckney:* 112 packages merchandise, 5 packages merchandise, 4 packages merchandise.
From same warehouse, imported per *Justitia,* London: 2 packages merchandise, 2 packages merchandise.
From same warehouse, imported per *Goodhue,* New York: 66 coils rope.
From same warehouse, imported per *Delta,* Halifax: 2 packages merchandise.
From same warehouse, imported per *Prima Donna,* London: 4 packages merchandise.
From Smith Island warehouse, imported per *Agrippina,* London: 600 packages merchandise.
From Higgs and Hyland's warehouse, imported per *Carl Emil,* Liverpool: 1 package merchandise.
From Johnson and Croft's warehouse, imported per *F. Drake:* 2 packages merchandise.

Virgin, about 291 tons, St. George's for Nassau, June 14, 1864, 1864, Robert C. Halpin, master:

1 iron horn and ship stores.

Atalanta, about 258 tons, St. George's for Nassau, June 20, 1864, M. P. Usina, master:

Imported per *Melina:* 20 cases bacon.
Imported per *Bonnie Belle:* 44 bundles iron ties.
6 cases merchandise.

Mary Celestia, about 207 tons, St. George's for Nassau, June 20, 1864, N. E. Green, master:

From Musson's stores: 76 bales and cases merchandise, 2 cases merchandise, 1 case merchandise, 2 casks hams, 1 bale merchandise.
From Johnson and Croft's stores: 38 casks—68 cases bacon.

City of Petersburg, about 420 tons, St. George's for Nassau, June 25, 1864, F. W. Fuller, master:

From Higgs and Hyland's warehouse, imported per *Carl Emil* and *Prima Donna:* 6 cases stationery, 13 cases merchandise, 1 cask merchandise.

Duty paid at Hamilton: 1 bale bunting.

From Higgs and Hyland's warehouse: 250 bundles iron hoops.

From Penno's warehouse: 20 cases tin.

Transferred from *Old Dominion:* 3 cases merchandise.

1 case, 1 trunk boots, 1 trunk wearing apparel.

Rouen, about 165 tons, St. George's for Nassau, June 28, 1864, Lawrence Marshall, master:

From Penno's warehouse, imported per *Nebula* (1): 100 cases tea.

From Musson's warehouse, imported per *Nebula* (2): 100 cases hoop iron.

From Higgs and Hyland's warehouse, imported per *Ocean Sprite:* 1 case merchandise, 1 bale merchandise.

From warehouse, imported per *Harriet Pinckney:* 100 sacks saltpeter, 31 cases shoes, 1 bale blankets, 2 casks sugar.

From Fisher's warehouse, imported per *Pevensey:* 3 casks whiskey.

From Musson's warehouse, imported per *Arbutus:* 8 cases brandy.

Per purchase account: 5 casks wine, 2 cases leather.

Little Hattie, about 246 92/100 tons, St. George's for Nassau, June 30, 1864, Jesse DeHorsey, master:

200 sacks saltpeter, 15 casks hardware, 16 casks hardware, 6 casks hardware, 2 casks curry combs, 1 cask hardware, 4 casks steel, 1 case steel, 50 barrels provisions, 19 cases stationery, 11 cases stationery, 5 cases fluid, 1 case merchandise, 13 cases leather, 2 cases carbines, 1 case sabers, 21 cases merchandise, 8 cases cavalry equipments, 1 case merchandise, 6 bales twine, 1 roll rubber packing, 50 bales cartridge paper, 120 pigs lead, 6 bales bagging, 25 coils rope, 1 case merchandise, 6 bales shirts, 9 cases merchandise.

Lilian, about 246 92/100 tons, St. George's for Nassau, July 1, 1864, D. S. Martin, master:

62 bundles sheet iron, 7 casks hardware, 2 casks block tin, 2 cases tin plates, 2 cases zinc, 2 cases merchandise, 1 bale merchandise, 5 bales blankets, 1 case stationery, 1 cask hardware, 25 bundles steel, 2 cases hardware, 13 bundles tubes, 68 bundles iron, 24 sheets iron, 2 kegs hardware, 1 cask merchandise, 1 cask paint, 7 boxes glass, 5 cases shoes, 16 bundles shovels, 2 bundles wire, 12 bundles rope, 178 kegs bicarbonate soda, 6 bales regatta shirts.

Boston, about 320 tons, St. George's for Nassau, July 2, 1864,
John B. Carron, master:

From Penno's warehouse, imported per *Nebula:* 24 barrels copperas.
From Fisher's warehouse, imported per *Nebula:* 465 sacks salt.
180 boxes soap, ships stores.

Florie, about 215 tons, St. George's for Nassau, July 2, 1864,
Henry S. Leffy, master:

From warehouse: 5 cases, 130 bags saltpeter, 5 cases, 68 cases rifles,
1 case merchandise, 1 case, 9 cases, 1 case.
Said not to be from warehouse: 6 bales.
From warehouses: 2 cases cotton cards, 80 pigs lead.
1 case, 3 cases.

Mary Celestia, about 207 tons, St. George's for Nassau, July
6, 1864, W. G. Green master:

From Musson's warehouse, imported per *Harkaway,* value £3,019.2.10:
12 cases merchandise, 44 bales merchandise, 34 casks bacon, 2 half
chests tea, 1 barrel sugar.
½ barrel coffee, 1 box merchandise, 5 boxes soap, 1 barrel whiskey.

Lynx, about 233 tons, St. George's for Nassau, July 8, 1864,
P. C. Reid, master:

From Hunter's and Penno's warehouses: 300 pigs lead, 150 sacks
saltpeter, 2 hogsheads sugar, 30 cases rifles, 4 cases pistols, 5 cases
steel.

Atalanta, about 253 tons, St. George's for Nassau, July 11,
1864, M. P. Usina, master:

From warehouse, imported per *Estaphania:* 700 cases preserved boiled
beef.
From warehouse, imported per *Sir George Flynn:* 50 casks bacon.

Edith, about 239 tons, St. George's for [Nassau?], July 22,
1864, L. Murray, master:

From Higgs anad Hyland's stores: 6 cases merchandise.
From John T. Bourne's warehouse: 1 cask whiskey.
From Hunter's warehouse: 20 bales cloth.
From Penno's warehouse: 17 cases merchandise, 2 casks merchandise, 1 case merchandise, 86 boxes bacon, 1 case merchandise, 1 case
linens, 6 barrels porter, 6 barrels ale, 6 cases brandy, 3 cases claret,
2 cases champagne, 2 cases port wine, 6 cases sherry wine, 1 cask
soda water.
54 barrels onions.

Advance, about 430 tons, St. George's for Nassau, July 25, 1864, Joannes Wyllie, master:

From Penno's warehouse, imported per *J. W.:* 1 cask.
From same warehouse, imported per *Ann & Mary:* 12 casks, 8 bales leather, 25 boxes bacon.
From same warehouse, imported per *Jane Smith:* 100 bales logwood, 10 barrels copperas, 10 barrels alum, 20 kegs blue stones, 42 bales cloth.
From same warehouse, imported per *Harkaway:* 32 cases.
From Hunter's warehouse, imported per *Arbutus:* 1 case.

Alice, about 803 tons, St. George's for Nassau, July 25, 1864, C. B. Grant, master:

Imported per *Mary Garland (Colombo),* duty paid, value £5,200: 174 packages merchandise.
From Hunter's warehouse, imported per *Glendower:* 200 sacks saltpeter.
From same warehouse, imported per *Harriet Pinckney:* 29 pigs lead.
From Fisher's warehouse, imported per *Pevensey:* 7 casks whiskey.

Helen, about 342 tons, St. George's for Nassau, July 25, 1864, J. A. Waddell, master:

Imported per *Caroline Goodyear,* not landed: 15 cases merchandise, 5 cases zinc, 14 cases tins, 515 bars steel.

Little Hattie, about 246 tons, St. George's for Nassau, July 25, 1864, Henry S. Leffy, master:

Outward cargo reported June 30, 1864, having returned in want of coal.[1]

Mary Bowen, about 225 tons, St. George's for Nassau, July 26, 1864, Jesse DeHorsey, master:

33 cases merchandise, 25 cases merchandise, 13 cases merchandise, 5 cases merchandise, 12 cases merchandise, 7 casks merchandise, 15 cases twine, 3 packages.

Flamingo, about 283 tons, St. George's for Nassau, July 28, 1864, Atkinson, master:

Inward cargo, and: 8 packages merchandise, 6 cases ale, 2 cases brandy, 2 cases sherry.

---

[1]This indicates that the *Little Hattie* tried to run the blockade, but was unable to do so and had to return to St. George's.

Mary Celestia, about 207 tons, St. George's for Nassau, August 2, 1864, Arthur Sinclair, master:

From J. W. Musson's warehouse, imported per *Levant:* 392 barrels pork, 27 bales blankets (duty paid, value £1,864.10.11).

From same warehouse, imported per *J. W.:* 1 tierce hams, 1 case glass pipes, 1 bale clothing, 1 bale clothing.

Chicora, about 599 tons, St. George's for Nassau, August 8, 1864, P. C. Carigs, master:

From Hunter's warehouse, imported per *J. W.:* 47 cases boots, 3 cases boots, 17 cases boots, 6 bales blankets, 1 bale blankets, 3 bales cloths, 7 bales cloths.

Duty paid: 31 barrels sugar, 29 barrels sugar, 27 barrels sugar.

From Higgs and Hyland's warehouse, imported per *Alpha:* 1 barrel blue stone.

25 coils manilla rope, 1 box merchandise, 1 box merchandise, 2 boxes merchandise, 1 box merchandise, 2 boxes merchandise.

Ella, about 404 tons, St. George's for Nassau, August 9, 1864, C. J. Barkley, master:

From Hunter's warehouse, imported per *Maria Victoria:* 49 cases boots and shoes, 4 cases stationery, 6 hogsheads gin, 1 case calfskins, 1 case calfskins, 2 barrels lamp black, 2 barrels lampblack, 124 octaves brandy, 10 firkins wine, 1 box bonnet frames, 49 cases tea, 21 cases dry goods, 5 bags pimento, 20 bags pepper, 10 hogsheads olive oil, 1 case brushes and combs.

From *Colombo*, imported per *Mary Garland*, duty paid on value £1,762.10.6: 1 case linen, 1 case jaconets, 1 case cloth, 1 case calfskins, 11 bales bagging, 20 casks alcohol, 10 bales gunny bagging, 6 barrels linseed oil.

14 boxes tins, 3 cases plies, 7 cases steel, 1 case steel, 1 cask cutlery, 9 casks tins, 38 bundles sheet iron, 7 coils rope, 11 cases hats, 5 casks linseed oil, 100 boxes soap, 30 boxes starch, 75 kegs soda, 2 bales dry goods, 60 barrels herrings, 60 barrels sulphur, 16 barrels leather, 10 cases drugs, 9 cases boots and shoes, 50 bundles paper, 24 cases kerosene oil, 62 kegs bicarbonate of soda, 5 barrels lard oil, 3 bales twine, 7 barrels glue, 11 bolt bales skirting.

Wando, about 650 tons, St. George's for Nassau, August 26, 1864, H. Holgate, master:

From Hunter's warehouse, imported per *J. W.:* 22 bales cloth, 15 bales blankets, 1 bale blankets, 2 bales cloths, 13 bales cloths, 15 bales blankets, 1 bale cloth, 9 cases boots [books?], 2 cases boots, 4 cases boots, 15 cases boots, 18 cases boots, 3 cases boots, 7 cases boots, 13 cases boots,[2] 8 bales blankets, 15 bales cloths, 10 bales cloths.

Imported per *Arbutus*, duty paid, value £665.10: 10 cases (amount of duty to be drawn back, £13.6.2).

50 barrels crushed sugar, 50 boxes soap, 4 cases calfskins, 10 cases shirting, 1 barrel blue stone, 50 coils manilla rope, 2 boxes tea.

Lynx, about 233 tons, St. George's for Nassau, August 30, 1864:

From Hunter's warehouse: 200 sacks saltpeter, 100 bales cartridges.

From Higgs and Hyland's warehouse: 1 barrel blue stone.

Amelia Ann, about 77 tons, St. George's for Nassau, September 19, 1864, C. L. Millard, master:

75 bags coffee	£379. 12. 8
6 barrels whiskey	68. 0. 0
	£447. 12. 8

Talisman, about 173 tons, St. George's for Nassau, September 28, 1864, Thomas S. Gilpin, master:

66 pieces forming a cotton press, 8 packages sundries, 100 sacks saltpeter, 43 bales merchandise.

Virginia, about 456 tons, St. George's for Nassau, September 29, 1864, Thomas J. Moore, master:

From J. W. Musson's warehouse, imported per *Mystery:* 214 half chests tea.

From same warehouse, imported per *Convoy:* 182 boxes bacon.

From same warehouse, imported per *Powerful:* 9 boxes bacon.

From same warehouse, imported per *J. W.:* 100 cases vegetables, 19 cases soap.

Imported per *Thomas Edwards:* 150 boxes bacon.

Imported per *Solway Queen:* 523 bundles hoop iron.

151 cases shoes.

Christina Jacqueline, about 155 tons, St. George's for Nassau, October 22, 1864, Richard Squire, master:

From Penno's warehouse, imported per *Aurora:* 72 casks bottles, 97 cases paper, 5 cases paper, 10 cases paper, 4 cases paper, 262 packages drugs, 3 packages drugs.

---

[2]All of these items listed as boots may have been books. The writing is not clear.

Little Hattie, about 246 tons, St. George's for Nassau, October 25, 1864, Henry S. Leffy, master:

771 packages merchandise.

Caroline, about 403 tons, St. George's for Nassau, October [25?], 1864, L. M. Hudgins, master:

From hulk *Colombo,* imported per *Mary Garland,* duty paid, value £6,049.9.6: 387 packages merchandise.

From J. Musson's warehouse, imported per *Arbutus:* 20 cases brandy.

From Fisher's warehouse, imported per *Pevensey:* 8 casks whiskey.

From J. Musson's warehouse, imported per *Sylph:* 3 casks hardware, 1 case hardware.

Imported per *Thomas Edwards:* 2 cases merchandise, 5 bundles sheet iron, 18 casks copper, 4 bundles copper bolts, 8 casks ingot tin, 7 casks pig lead, 8 casks spelter, 7 cases zinc, 6 cases, 10 bundles sheet lead.

From Hunter's warehouse, imported per *Convoy:* 100 bundles iron ties.

Owl, about 330 tons, St. George's for Nassau, October 29, 1864, John W. Dunnington, master:

508 packages merchandise.

Mattie Banks, about 525 tons, St. George's for Nassau, October 29, 1864, George Bevin, master:

710 tons coal.

A. E. Fry, about 372 tons, St. George's for Nassau, October 31, 1864, Joseph Fry, master:

158 barrels sugar, 173 boxes bacon, 126 tierces beef, 18 cases stationery, 40 coils rope.

"This Cargo was cleared from Hamilton 29th August. A portion of it was thrown overboard at sea, exact quantity not ascertained."

Talisman, about 173 tons, St. George's for Nassau, November 1, 1864, John Knox, master:

4 bales bagging, 1 bale twine, 220 cases rifles.

John Henry, about 511 tons, St. George's for Nassau, November 4, 1864, D. McSpooner, master:

From Johnson and Croft's warehouse, imported per *Powerful:* 36 hogsheads alcohol, 233 barrels pork, 20 casks cement.

From same warehouse, imported per *Mavronendales* [?]: 418 barrels pork, 13 bales leather, 4 cases merchandise, 1 cask merchandise, 111 bundles sheet iron, 592 sacks salt.

A quantity of old iron.

Leonard Berry, about 200 tons, St. George's for Nassau, November 9, 1864, Joseph Steele, master:

Inward cargo outward.

96 cases merchandise, 39 bales merchandise, 56 cases merchandise, 3 bales merchandise, 2 bales sacks, 65 bales cloth, 17 bales flannel, 14 bales blankets, 20 cases boots, 10 cases boots, 296 pigs lead, 17 cases paper, 43 casks bottles, 2 trusses bottles, 40 packages apothecaries ware.

Alert, about 62 tons, St. George's for Nassau, November 14, 1864, A. G. Newman, master:

From Johnson's warehouse, imported per *Powerful:* 32 barrels compo [?], 12 barrels coating.

From same warehouse, imported per *Mavronendales* [?]: 4 cases merchandise, 33 bales harness hides, 36 casks alcohol (1977 gallons).

Virginia, about 456 tons, St. George's for Nassau, November 15, 1864, Thomas J. Moore, master:

From J. W. Musson's stores, imported per *Thomas Edwards:* 234 boxes bacon.

From M. Frith's stores, imported per *Powerful:* 31 boxes bacon.

From J. W. Musson's stores, imported per *Emily Agnes:* 53 casks bacon.

From W. H. Gosling's stores, imported per *Emily Agnes:* 500 bundles hoop iron, 30 bales gunny cloth.

From "Mr Cs" *[Mary Celestia ?]:* 23 casks bacon, wrecked goods.

Imported per *Mary Bond:* 1 box medicines.

Armstrong, about 214 tons, St. George's for Nassau, November 23, 1864, Charles Nelson, master:

Per entry: 10 bales gunny cloth, 200 bundles iron hoops, 1370 cases preserved meats.

From Penno's warehouse, imported per *Harkaway:* 5 crates earthenware.

Emma Henry, about 242 tons, St. George's for Nassau, November 23, 1864, P. C. Reid, master:

8 cases merchandise, 17 ingots tin, 2 cases steel, 14 bales gunny cloth, 1 box quinine, 2 half barrels coffee, 12 boxes candles, 7 cases merchandise, 100 cases candles, 4 cases merchandise, 1 barrel merchandise, 4 cases merchandise, 28 packages machinery (part inward cargo), 130 sacks saltpeter, 30 cases rifles, 50 cases shoes, 10 barrels alcohol, 10 barrels sperm oil, 5 barrels linseed oil, 5 bales blankets, 1 package merchandise, 2 barrels whiskey, 7 cases merchandise, 1 reel wire, 10 carboys acid.

Mary, about 124 tons, St. George's for Nassau, November 24, 1864, M. Collier, master:

> 3 packages merchandise, 4 bundles canvas, 2 cases merchandise, 3 cases merchandise.

Ann and Mary, about 145 tons, St. George's for Nassau, November 24, 1864, Abraham Jones, master:

> "Inward cargo from Liverpool not landed here."
> 220 tons coal.

Vulture, about 335 tons, St. George's for Nassau, November 26, 1864, W. G. Green, master:

> From Penno's warehouse, imported per *Nebula:* 107 cases vegetable food.
> From same warehouse, imported per *Queen of Britain:* 5 bales cloth.
> From Fisher's warehouse, imported per *Harkaway:* 350 kegs soda.
> From Johnson's warehouse, imported per *Ann and Mary:* 1 truss carpeting, 43 bundles spades, 1 box borax, 37 boxes glass.
> From Higgs and Hyland's warehouse, imported per *Francis Drake:* 4 bales blankets.
> From same warehouse, imported per *Goodyear:* 3 cases merchandise.
> 2 barrels wire, 4 barrels wire, 1 case tacks, 2 casks wire, 1 case merchandise, 2 cases merchandise, 4 cases skins, 9 barrels leather, 10 cases shoes, 4 cases shoes, 1 box merchandise, 2 bales merchandise, 1 chest tea, 12 bales candles, 1 trunk merchandise, 1 trunk merchandise, 1 bale blankets, 2 cases merchandise, 30 cases merchandise.

Vixen, about 305 tons, St. George's for Nassau, November 28, 1864, T. M. Walton, master:

> From Penno's warehouse, imported per *Nebula:* 107 cases vegetable food.
> From same warehouse, imported per *Queen of Britain:* 5 bales cloth.
> From Fisher's warehouse, imported per *Harkaway:* 20 casks soda ash, 74 kegs soda.
> From Johnson's warehouse, imported per *Francis Drake:* 3 bales blankets.
> 30 cases merchandise, 10 bales blankets, 4 cases merchandise.

Stag, about 299 tons, St. George's for Nassau, December 1, 1864, John Burroughs, master:

> Imported per *Mary Bond:* 75 cases shoes, 7 bales woolens.
> Imported per *Blink Bonny:* 30 cases merchandise.
> Imported per *Diana:* 25 cases merchandise.
> Imported per *Jane Goodyear:* 2 cases merchandise.

Imported per *Harkaway:* 5 tons pig iron.
Imported per *Harriet Pinckney:* 130 sacks saltpeter.
Inward cargo outward, 54 packages.

Juno, about 230 tons, St. George's for Nassau, December 2, 1864, Charles F. Williams, master:

Imported per *Sylph,* October 6, duty paid: 250 tierces beef.
129 tierces beef, 352 barrels pork, 630 cases preserved meats, 100 tierces beef, 100 barrels pork, 104 tierces beef, 100 tierces beef, 264 tierces beef, 950 cases preserved meats, 68 barrels pork.

Talisman, about 173 tons, St. George's for Nassau, December 3, 1864, John Knox, master:

30 cases merchandise, 5 tons pig iron, 33 cases shoes, 12 cases shoes, 29 cases shoes, 5 cases shoes, 33 bales merchandise, 3 bales merchandise, 1 bale merchandise, 100 sacks saltpeter.

Harkaway, about 658 tons, St. George's for Nassau, December 5, 1864, Joseph Cundy, master:

Imported per *Militia,* duty paid, value £50.0.0: 427 tons coal.
4 crates merchandise, 20 casks merchandise, 1 case merchandise, 171 packages merchandise, 36 anvils, 20 bales, 130 bales, 209 packages blankets, 140 cases boots, 32 cases machinery, 28 casks screws, 44 cases boots, 8 bales cloth, 2 bales flannel, 40 cases cotton cards, 48 cases shoes, 1 case samples, 1 bale flannel, 99 cases brandy, 104 coils rope, 115 coils rope.

Princess Royal, about 103 tons, St. George's for Nassau, December 14, 1864, T. D. Newbold, master:

2 bales cotton waste, 2 cases cheese, 1 case fruit, 10 bags coffee, 46 cases oil, 81 bales bagging, 1 boat, 14 floats [?], 11 barrels porter, 1 barrel ale, 6 cases wine, 224 bundles, 356 plates, 107 sheets iron, 5 casks brandy, 5 rolls matting, 1 iron safe, 2 pianos, 2 boxes harmoniums, 25 cases merchandise, 173 barrels potatoes.

Josephine, about .... tons, St. George's for St. John's, N.B., December 17, 1864, J. Slocomb, master:

Ballast &c.
Imported per *Hans Rude,* duty paid: 1400 sacks salt.

Pleiades, about 330 tons, St. George's for Nassau, December 20, 1864, William Knowlton, master:

From W. H. Gosling's stores (bonded September 6, 1864), imported per *Solway Queen:* 573 tierces beef, 745 barrels pork, 65 cases preserved vegetables, 125 cases preserved meats.

From same store (bonded October 4, 1864), imported per *Emily Agnes:* 418 tierces beef, 400 barrels pork, 66 cases beef juice, 22 cases preserved soup, 9 cases preserved beef.

From J. W. Musson's warehouse (bonded October 4, 1864), imported per *Queen of Clippers:* 944 cases preserved meat.

From same warehouse (bonded July 13, 1864), imported per *J. W.:* 196 cases vegetables.

From same warehouse (bonded November 1, 1864), imported per *Wanderer:* 345 cases preserved beef.

Eleanor, about 298 tons, St. George's for Nassau, December 22, 1864, Thomas Campbell, master:

Inward cargo consisting of 3769 packages merchandise.

From J. W. Musson's warehouse, imported per *Wanderer:* 500 cases preserved beef.

From Johnson's warehouse: 49 barrels whiskey, 10 cases merchandise.

Susan Bume, about 445 tons, St. George's for Nassau, December 24, 1864, D. S. Martin, master:

Inward cargo from Glasgow.

50 cases shoes, 40 cases shoes, 60 boxes bacon, 3 bundles leather, 2 casks merchandise, 41 bales merchandise, 19 bales merchandise, 70 barrels copperas, 30 barrels copperas, 1 case merchandise, 11 boxes merchandise, 2 barrels sugar, 3 half barrels sugar, 3 cases merchandise, 3 cases merchandise, 12 cases merchandise, 8 cases merchandise, 1 bale merchandise, 2 bales merchandise, 30 coils rope, 13 cases merchandise, 2 barrels merchandise, 2 packages merchandise, 1 case merchandise, 1 bag coffee, 6 bales merchandise.

Levanter, about 551 tons, St. George's for St. John's, N.B., December 27, 1864, D. W. Corning, master:

Duty paid: 1769 sacks salt.

Owl, about 450 tons, St. George's for Nassau, January 3, 1865, J. N. Maffitt, master:

50 cases merchandise, 26 cases merchandise, 2 cases merchandise, 2 cases merchandise, 1 case merchandise, 10 cases merchandise, 2 bales merchandise, 20 cases merchandise, 1 case merchandise, 1 case merchandise, 4 cases hardware, 3 casks hardware, 30 cases merchandise, 130 sacks saltpeter, 200 pigs lead, 24 packages hardware, 4 casks hardware, 3 cases merchandise, 100 bundles hoop iron.

Leonard Berry, about 200 tons, St. George's for Nassau, January 9, 1865, Joseph D. Steele, master:

19 cases, 24 bales, 94 cases, 16 casks, 24 cases, 34 tierces, 30 crates, 4 cases, 8 cases, 114 bales, 301 cases, 9 casks, 2 crates, 3 cases, 60 bales,

300 cases, 40 casks, 17 casks, 167 casks, 2 casks, 3 crates, 525 bags saltpeter.

Alert, about 61 tons, St. George's for Nassau, January 13, 1865, Robert T. Ingham, master:

50 tons coal (£50.0.0.), 49 packages merchandise.

Stag, about 417 tons, St. George's for Nassau, January 14, 1865, Richard H. Gayle, master:

130 sacks saltpeter, 7 casks lead, 5 packages merchandise, 32 cases boots and pegwood, 59 bales merchandise, 3 cases merchandise, 30 cases merchandise, 5 hogsheads shoes, 2 cases shoes, 14 bales blankets.

Charlotte, about 403 tons, St. George's for Nassau, January 14, 1865, Thomas E. Cocker, master:

166 pigs lead, 13 cases wines.

From Hunter's warehouse: 130 sacks saltpeter, 16 cases steel, 100 bundles iron ties, 50 cases merchandise, 2 casks hardware, 2 pieces castings, 3 cases machinery, 1 bag glue, 1 bottle quicksilver, 16 packages merchandise, 2 cases merchandise, 6 cases merchandise, 44 cases merchandise, 3 bales hosiery, 8 bales blankets, 18 bales blankets, 2 bales blankets, 5 bales woolens, 13 bales blankets, 31 boxes cloth, 1 case boots, 11 cases buttons, 19 cases shoes, 29 cases shoes.

Purchased: 1 bale blankets, 12 boxes candles, 2 half chests tea, 2 boxes mustard, 3 cases boots, 1 iron safe, 7 cases merchandise, 3 tierces, 4 packages.

From Smith Island warehouse: 200 cases merchandise.

Imported per *Nebula:* 200 bundles hoop iron.

From Higgs and Hyland's warehouse, imported per *Hawk:* 4 cases merchandise.

From Penno's warehouse; 30 coils rope.

From same warehouse, imported per *Queen of Britain:* 30 bales cloth.

From R. Higgs' warehouse, imported per *Lady Milne:* 2 cases hats.

Whisper, about 438 tons, St. George's for Nassau, January 18, 1865, William A. Webb, master:

Inward cargo consisting of 1979 packages merchandise.
71 boxes bacon.

Rattlesnake, about 259 tons, St. George's for Nassau, January 19, 1865, M. P. Usina, master:

Inward cargo consisting of 1531 packages merchandise.
From W. H. Gosling's warehouse: 504 bags coffee.

Chameleon, about 575 tons, St. George's for Nassau, January 19, 1865, John Wilkinson, master:

From John T. Bourne's warehouse: 6 bales blankets, 1 half bale blankets.

From Crenshaw: 40 boxes bacon.

From Greg: 14 boxes bacon, 19 casks bacon.

7 cases zinc, 10 bundles lead, 18 casks copper, 3 coils wire, 1 case merchandise, 20 bales clothing, 9 bales clothing, 17 bales clothing, 5 bales clothing.

Lady Milne, about 304 tons, St. George's for Nassau, January 20, 1865, Thomas M. Dill, master:

From Gosling's warehouse, imported per *Emily Agnes:* 530 barrels pork.

From same warehouse, imported per *Solway Queen:* 441 bags coffee.

From Musson's warehouse, imported per *Albion:* 442 cases preserved meats.

From same warehouse, imported per *Wanderer:* 623 cases preserved meat.

From same warehouse, imported per *Mystery:* 250 tierces beef.

From same warehouse, imported per *Queen of Clippers:* 14 cases preserved meat.

Duty paid, £4,381.0.0 2261 cases preserved meat.

Shipped by D. Kanwishler [?]: 28 cases merchandise, 20 bales merchandise (duty paid), 6 casks blue stone.

Florence, about 469 tons, St. George's for Nassau, January 24, 1865, Samuel De Forest, master:

Per entry: 504 bags coffee, 600 barrels pork.

Virginia, about 456 tons, St. George's for Nassau, January 25, 1865, D. H. Watson, master:

Per entry: 504 bags coffee, 700 barrels pork.

Deer, about 300 tons, St. George's for Nassau, January 26, 1865, Joannes Wyllie, master:

Reported in inward entry of January 13, 1865, and not taken out of vessel here: 123 packages merchandise.

Owl, about 450 tons, St. George's for Nassau, January 26, 1865, J. N. Maffitt, master:

Inward cargo out, entered January 21, 1865.

Isabella Maria, about 67 tons, St. George's for Nassau, January 28, 1865, W. H. Williams, master:

From warehouse, Hamilton: 27 bundles sheet iron, 31 cases merchandise.

From McCallan's warehouse: 48 bales bagging.

From *Chebucto* [?]: 19 cases boots and shoes.

Duty paid, £225.0.0: 15 cases boots and shoes.

2 trunks merchandise, 794 sheets iron, 274 bundles hoop iron, 100 kegs rivets, 104 single tubes, 108 bundles tubes, 4 hogsheads beef, 1 cask porter, 1 cask ale, 1 case drugs, 2 cases drugs, 1 case drugs, 100 barrels potatoes (foreign, £50.0.0.).

Loda, about 420 tons, St. George's for Nassau, February 23, 1865, Henry Wade, master:

1950 cases preserved meats, 20 barrels porter, 21 barrels oil, 8 barrels tallow, 2 chloride lime, 2 soda crystals, 1 tierce hams, 8 barrels blue stone, 12 tierces soda ash, 1 cask bichrome [?], 63 plates spelter, 200 bundles iron ties, 100 kegs bicarbonate soda, 52 bales gunny cloth, 200 boxes soap, 295½ chests tea, 432 bags Rio coffee, 4 cases stationery, 240 bales oakum, 12 barrels crushed sugar, 8 old sails, 1 tarpaulin, 6 wheelbarrows, 300 tons coal, 75 cases shoes.

Europa, about 297 tons, St. George's for Nassau, February 24, 1865, Jacob Utley, master:

126 cases bacon, 567 barrels pork, 120 cases preserved vegetables, 157 tierces beef, 1000 cases preserved beef, 78 cases preserved vegetables, 62 cases soup and bouillon, 33 cases preserved boiled beef, 40 cases preserved vegetables, 33 cases vegetables, 67 cases beef juice, 1 case knives, 117 cases preserved beef, 5 cases knives, 214 cases preserved meats, 23 cases preserved soup, 947 cases boiled beef, 200 bundles iron ties, 2 cases sundries, 1 case glass, 4 reels telegraph wire, 1 case merchandise, 8 cases stationery, 1 cask stationery, 2 cases hardware, 46 cases glass, 2 bales merchandise, 1 case wire, 5 bundles sheet iron, 1 keg rivets, 1 keg putty, 6 barrels fire clay, 3 crates crockery, 21 bales cloth, 25 bales blankets, 7 bales gunny bagging, 237 bags Rio coffee, 341 bags Rio coffee, 217 furnace bars, 1 milner's iron safe, 1 milner's chest, 1 box containing a desk, 3 bundles segs. [?], 1 rack for desk, 3 old sails, 24 wheelbarrows, 6 trucks, 1 set upright scales.

City of Richmond, about 459 tons, St. George's for Nassau, February 25, 1865, W. Scott, master:

Portion of inward cargo.

"Stores for ship's use, bought and duty paid here": 1 box oxtail soup, 2 boxes sea salmon, 5 boxes bottled (fruit), 2 boxes mock turtle, 1 box harricott mutton, 1 box vegetable soup, 1 case sherry, 2 boxes worcestershire sauce, 14 boxes preserved potatoes, 11 boxes porter, 10 boxes ale, 1 box brast [?] mutton, 1 box hare soup, 2 jars tripe, 1 jar lime juice, 3 packages mustard, 3 bags salt, 1 keg tongues.

435 barrels pork, 9 tierces beef, 11 carboys acid.

Louisa Ann Fanny, about 425 tons, St. George's for Havana, March 8, 1865, W. G. Pinchon, master:

Inward cargo in transit.

Also: 300 sacks saltpeter, 113 cases rifles, 100 cases merchandise, 8 cases revolvers, 100 bales cartridge paper.

Louisa Ann Fanny, about 425 tons, St. George's for Havana, April 8, 1865, W. G. Pinchon, master:

From W. L. Penno's warehouse, imported per *Gladiator,* Liverpool, August, 1862: 215 packages hardware, 39 cases merchandise.

From same warehouse, imported per *Harriet Pinckney,* London, June, 1863: 10 cases hardware.

From same warehouse, imported per *Justitia,* January, 1863: 51 casks hardware.

From Todd's stores, imported per *Lemuella,* London, August, 1863: 119 bales merchandise, 58 casks and boxes hardware.

From Hunter's warehouse, imported per *Eitea,* Liverpool: 502 boxes tin.

From same warehouse, imported per *Chameleon:* 571 bales blankets and clothing.

From same warehouse, imported per *Convoy:* 1 bale twine, 58 coils rope, 8 cases merchandise.

From same warehouse, imported per *Goodhue,* New York: 96 coils rope.

From same warehouse, imported per *Hyppolite,* Liverpool: 1000 sacks saltpeter, 2005 pigs lead.

From Higgs and Hyland's warehouse, imported per *Queen of Clippers:* 7 casks shoes.

From Musson's warehouse, imported per *Eleanor,* Liverpool: 2 cases clothing.

From John T. Bourne's warehouse, imported per *Alexandra,* Liverpool: 1 case cutlery.

From Hunter's warehouse, imported per *Jane Goodyear* and *Bonnie Belle:* 8 cases clothing.

From Smith Island warehouse, imported per *Harriet Pinckney:* 60 boxes cartridges.

From same warehouse, imported per *Miriam:* 140 boxes cartridges.

Imported per *Coral Isle:* 7 casks.

Imported per *Queen of Clippers:* 1 case clothing.

From J. Johnson's warehouse: 3 cases merchandise.

21 casks hardware, 25 barrels alcohol (750 gallons), 2 bales numnahs.

Index

McHugh, B. & E., 45
McHugh, James, 41
McQueen, Capt. Alexander, 128
McRae, Colin J., Confederate financial agent, xxv, xxvi, xxvii, xxix, xli
McSpooner, Capt. D., 140
Madeira, Island of, 12, 31
Maffitt, Capt. J. N., 58, 132, 144, 146
Mallet, Col. John W., C.S.A., xxv, xxvi, xxxi, xl n91, 79, 88
Mallory, Stephen R., Confederate Secretary of the Navy, 60, 63
Manassas, battle of, xiii
Marshall, Capt. Lawrence, 125, 129, 131, 135
Martin, Capt. D. S., 135, 144
Mary, blockade runner, 142
Mary Bowen, blockade runner, 137
Mary Celestia, blockade runner, 131, 134, 136, 138
Mason, James M., Confederate Commissioner, xv, xxvi, xxx, 9, 52, 54
Massie, W. O., 51
Mattie Banks, blockade runner, 140
Memminger, Christopher G., Confederate Secretary of the Treasury, xviii, xx, 83
Memphis, blockade runner, 23, 24
Merrimac, blockade runner, xxxii, 27, 32, 34, 35, 38, 39, 111
Mexico, xl
Meyer, W. E., & Co., xxii
Milicent, blockade runner, 42
Millard, Capt. C. L., 139
Miller, Hugh, xlii, xliii, 107
Minho, blockade runner, 27, 69, 109
Minnie, blockade runner, 57, 60, 61, 62, 63, 128, 129
Miriam, steamer, 39, 40, 42, 44, 47, 76, 77, 84
Mitchell, C. T., & Co., 53
Mitchell, Mr., 12, 14, 15, 21
Mohican, U.S.S., 27
Moore, Gen. S. P., Surgeon General of Confederate Army, xxx, 78, 88
Moore, Capt. Thomas J., 139, 141
Morfit, Miss Fanny B., 84
Morfit, Maj. M., 84
Muney, Capt. Charles, 116
Murphy, Sir William, Governor of the Bahama Islands, xvi n17
Murray, Capt. C., 118
Murray, Capt. L., 136
Musson, A. J., 46
Musson, J. W., xxii, 40, 78, 93

Nashville, C.S.S., 8, 10, 19, 20
Nassau, blockade runner, xix
Nelly, blockade runner, 22
Nelson, Capt. Charles, 132, 141
Nesbitt, Lt. Gov. of the Bahama Islands, xvi n17
Newbold, Capt. D. T., 143
Newcastle, Duke of, xxxiv
Newman, Capt. A. G., 141
Nina, blockade runner, 124
Nola, steamer, 57
Nonsuch, blockade runner, 130
North Heath, blockade runner, 57, 63, 128
Nutfield, blockade runner, 125

Ouchette, blockade runner, 27
Overed, Gurney & Co., 27, 35, 38, 40
Owl, blockade runner, 140, 144, 146
Oxley, John Stewart, & Co., 50, 60

Page, Capt. D. J., 123
Parke, Capt. F. T., 27, 28, 31, 33, 69, 109
Parker, Harry, xlii, xliii, 107
Patros, blockade runner, 22
Patten, Capt. Alfred, 122
Patteson, Thomas A., 55
Pearson, Zachariah C., & Co., 16, 29, 30, 38, 40
Pegram, Lt., C. S. N., 10
Penguin, steamer, 24
Peniston, Capt. J., 132
Penno, W. L., xxii, 33, 83, 90, 93, 99, 100
Percussion caps, 80, 81, 86, 91, 92, 95, 99
Perry, Capt. Theo., 116
Pevensey, blockade runner, 130, 133
Phantom, blockade rupnner, xxxii, 84, 98, 117, 118
Phebe, steamer, 27, 34, 35, 38, 39
Phillips, Capt. F. B., 128
Pickering, Messrs., & Co., 77
Pierce, Franklin, xi
Pietsch, Edward, 44
Pinchon, Capt. W. G., 148
Pine, Capt., 67
Pleiades, blockade runner, 143
Porter, S. G., Confederate agent at Bermuda, xxii, 35, 36, 37, 39, 40, 84, 98, 111, 117, 118
Presto, blockade runner, 124
Prince Leopold, schooner, 5, 6
Princess Royal, blockade runner, 24, 143